CONTENTS

STOCKISTS AND SUPPLIERS

DMC cottons/floss:

DMC Creative World
Pullman Road
Wigston
Leicester LE18 2DY
UK

The DMC Corporation
Port Kearny
Building 10
South Kearny
New Jersey 07032
USA

DMC
51-66 Carrington Road
Marrickville
New South Wales 2204
Australia

Warnaar Trading
  Company Ltd
376 Ferry Road
PO Box 19567
Christchurch
New Zealand

S.A.T.C.
43 Somerset Road
PO Box 3868
Cape Town 8000
South Africa

Pebeo paints:

Pebeo UK
109 Solent Business Centre
Millbrook Road West
Millbrook
Southampton SO15 OHW
UK

Pebeo of America
Airport Road
PO Box 717
Swanton
VT 05488
USA

National Art
  Materials Pty Ltd
PO Box 678
Croydon
3136 Victoria
Australia

Pebeo Canada
1905 Roy Street
Sherbrooke
Quebec
Canada J1K 2X5

Liserfam Investments
  Pty Ltd
PO Box 1721
Bedfordview
2008 Johannesburg
South Africa

Lefranc et Bourgeois Textil paints:

ColArt Fine Art
  and Graphics
Whitefriars Avenue
Wealdstone
Harrow
Middlesex HA3 5RH
UK

ColArt Americas
11 Constitution Avenue
PO Box 1396
Piscataway
NJ 08855-1396
USA

Arjo Wiggins Pty Ltd
13-19 Keysborough Avenue
Keysborough
3173 Victoria
Australia

Maison 39
51 Ponsonby Road
PO Box 47184
Auckland
New Zealand

Ashley & Radmore
PO Box 57324
Johannesburg 2137
South Africa

ACKNOWLEDGMENTS

Photographs: Edward Allwright, Paul Bricknell, Alan Duns, Christine Hanscombe,
Gloria Nicol, Lizzie Orme, Steven Pam, Russell Sadur, Lucinda Symons,
Adrian Taylor, Shona Wood

Illustrations: Terry Evans, Sally Holmes, Coral Mula

Stencils by Tessa Brown. Stitches by Sheila Coulson

STITCH & STENCIL

Over 25 Easy Fabric-Based Projects

FOR CHILDREN

This edition published by Silverdale Books,
an imprint of Bookmart Ltd, in 2000

Bookmart Ltd
Desford Road,
Enderby,
Leicester LE9 5AD

Registered Number 2372865

Produced by Eaglemoss Publications
Based on *Needlecraft Magic*
Copyright © Eaglemoss Publications Ltd 2000

Printed in Italy

ISBN 1-85605-589-2

10 9 8 7 6 5 4 3 2 1

ELEPHANT PARADE

BRING THE MERRIMENT OF THE CIRCUS TO
YOUR NURSERY WITH THIS VERSATILE
STENCIL DESIGN. THE LARGER MOTIFS
MAKE EYECATCHING SOFT TOYS.

ELEPHANT MOBILE

Let your creative flair run riot when you make this mobile.
Cut out pieces from bright felts, join them with blanket
stitch and suspend them from dowelling.

YOU WILL NEED

- ❋ Two 16½in (42cm) lengths of wooden dowelling, ⅜in (10mm) in diameter
- ❋ Stencil
- ❋ Felt squares in pink, blue, red, lilac, orange and green
- ❋ DMC stranded cottons/floss as listed in colour key
- ❋ DMC soft cotton or wool
- ❋ Small bag of toy filling
- ❋ Packet of assorted sequins
- ❋ 12 small round beads
- ❋ One large wooden bead
- ❋ 16 coloured pompons, 1in (25mm) in diameter
- ❋ Wood adhesive
- ❋ Scissors
- ❋ Pins
- ❋ Turquoise emulsion/latex paint
- ❋ Paint brush
- ❋ Pinking shears
- ❋ Embroidery needle, size 5
- ❋ Craft knife
- ❋ Fabric marker or felt tip

COLOUR KEY

COLOURS		Skeins
	208 Purple	1
	704 Lime green	1
	740 Orange	1
	917 Pink purple	1
	5282 Metallic gold	1

The felt elephants are padded with toy filling and trimmed with shiny sequins attached with decorative metallic threads. They are suspended from stranded cottons (floss), embellished with pompons, and revolve on a dowelling cross-bar. You can buy the materials to make your mobile from craft shops, department stores and by mail order. Wooden dowelling can be purchased in 8ft (2.4m) lengths from do-it-yourself stores.

MAKING THE MOBILE

1 Working directly on to the felt, trace around the inside of the cutout of the sideways-facing adult elephant's body and ears. Join up the gaps created by the bridges to give a solid outline. Repeat the process on the different felts until you have six elephant fronts, six backs and 12 ears in a variety of colours. ▼

2 Cut out elephant shapes. Use pinking shears to cut out 12 diamond shapes 1½ x 1¼in (4 x 3cm) to make the backcloths. ▼

3 Using a contrasting or metallic cotton (floss), sew sequins on the backcloths, finishing the stitch on the right side with a small, decorative knot. Snip the thread to leave a short tail. Use all six strands of contrasting cotton (floss) to straight stitch a backcloth and two ears on to each body. Add beads for the eyes.

4 Pin two different coloured elephant shapes together. Blanket stitch in contrasting cotton (floss) around outer edges, leaving a small gap at the top to insert filling.

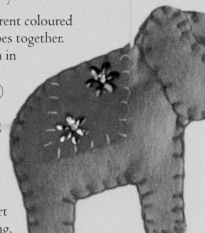

5 Pad the elephant and close the gap with blanket stitch. Using all six strands of cotton (floss), backstitch a 2in (5cm) tail to elephant. Knot end of tail. Following steps 1-5, make up five more elephants.

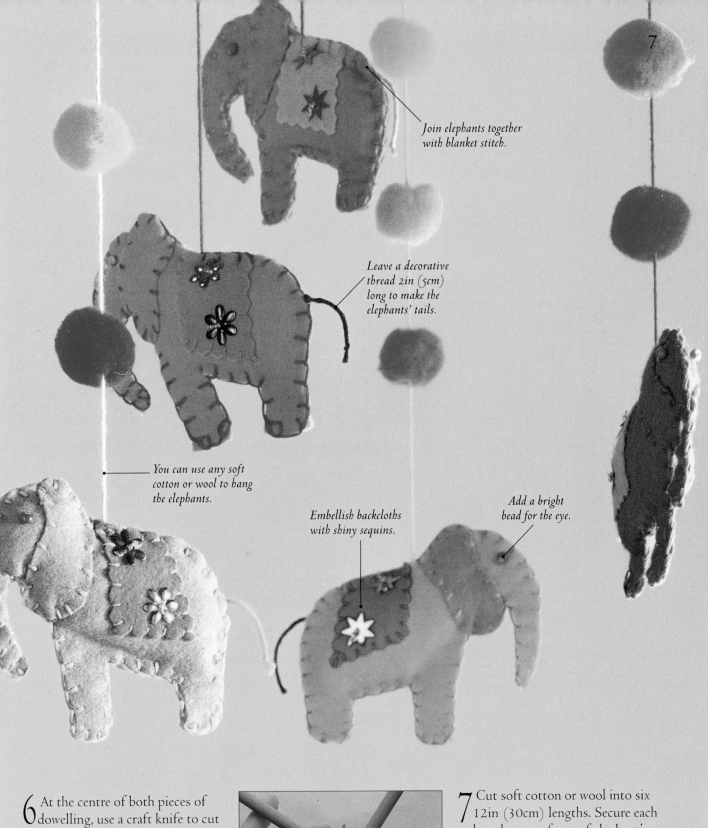

Join elephants together with blanket stitch.

Leave a decorative thread 2in (5cm) long to make the elephants' tails.

You can use any soft cotton or wool to hang the elephants.

Embellish backcloths with shiny sequins.

Add a bright bead for the eye.

6 At the centre of both pieces of dowelling, use a craft knife to cut a ⅜in (1cm) flat indent so that they sit comfortably as a cross-bar. Apply two coats of paint, leaving them to dry in between each coat. Glue the dowelling together with wood adhesive and allow to dry. Wind cotton round the join, thread on a bead and finish with a loop for hanging the mobile.▶

7 Cut soft cotton or wool into six 12in (30cm) lengths. Secure each length to top front of elephant's backcloth with a few backstitches. Thread pompons on to each length, tying a knot below each one to stop them slipping down the cotton. Glue a pompon to each end of the dowelling and tie on the elephants.

ELEPHANT PILLOWCASE

For a bold, coordinated room scheme, decorate pillowcases and duvet covers with a procession of adult and baby elephants. Stencil them in a single paint colour and add simple stitching to create an instant appliquéd effect. Blue fabric paint and orange bedlinen were used here, but you could choose other colours.

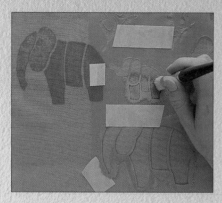

Using the stencil

For the pillowcase you will need the cutout sections shown in colour, the baby and the sideways-on adult elephant. Before you start, mask off rest of stencil.▶

Stencilling the elephants

Push card into top left-hand corner of pillowcase. Tape adult elephant cutout ¾in (2cm) in from the corner. Mix 1tbsp (15ml) of France Blue with a dab of White. Stencil motif. Leave to dry then stencil the baby elephant behind the adult. Fix dried paint with a hot iron. ◀

YOU WILL NEED

* Orange pillowcase
* Lefranc et Bourgeois Textil Paint in France Blue and White
* Stencil brush and stencil
* Masking tape
* Wallpaper lining paper
* Saucer
* Large piece of card
* Embroidery needle, size 5
* DMC stranded cottons/floss as listed in the colour key

COLOUR KEY

COLOURS	SKEINS
444 Yellow	1
606 Red	1
911 Green	1

Stitching the elephants

This idea for embroidering the elephants is so easy you could let your child try his or her hand at it. Use six strands of cotton (floss) throughout to outline the large elephant in red running stitches. Outline the backcloth with two rows of running stitch in yellow and add a fringe of straight stitches. Using green cotton (floss), work three rows of running stitch across the backcloth and add a cross stitch for the eye. Outline the small elephant in running stitch and yellow cotton (floss) and give it a green cross stitch eye.

BRIGHT IDEAS

ELEPHANT BADGE

Use the forward-facing elephant cutout to make a fun felt badge. Attached with a brooch pin (available from craft stores), it will dress up a school bag or denim jacket.

CHERUBS

INSPIRED BY PORTRAITS OF ANGELS,
CURLY-HAIRED CHERUBS FLOAT ON A
GAUZY CRIB DRAPE AND A SOFT
BABY QUILT.

CHERUB QUILT

YOU WILL NEED

- 1⅛yd (1m) of 56in (142cm) wide lightweight white cotton fabric
- Pebeo fabric paints in Fawn, Velvet Brown, Cornflower and White
- Stencil and stencil brush
- Kitchen paper and wallpaper lining paper
- Masking tape
- Tracing paper, pencil and dressmaker's carbon paper
- DMC stranded cottons/floss and metallic gold thread as listed in the colour key
- Embroidery needle, size 8
- Embroidery hoop
- 35 x 26¾in (89 x 68cm) of mediumweight washable polyester wadding/batting
- 26¾in (68cm) of ½in (12mm) wide pale blue satin ribbon
- White sewing thread

Angelic cherubs make the perfect decoration for a new baby's crib.

The delicate stitching on the ribbon-trimmed cherub panel combines gleaming stranded cottons (floss) and metallic gold thread for a subtle effect. The quilt shown here is 34 x 25½in (86 x 65cm), but you can adjust the size if you wish.

Preparing the stencil

The diagram (right) shows the complete cherub stencil. For the cherub quilt, you will be using the cherub leaning on his hands, and his hair, shown here in colour. As you work, mask off any cutouts close to the one you are using.

Preparing the fabric

From the white fabric: cut a 26¾ x 7½in (68 x 19cm) strip. Fold it in half widthwise and press the crease. Press a lengthwise crease 2½in (6.5cm) from one long edge. Tape the strip to the work surface with the long sides horizontal and the crease at the bottom.

STENCILLING THE CHERUBS

1 Mask off the wings. Position the cutout, with the head tilted to the left, so that the arms rest on the lengthwise crease with the left elbow 1½in (4cm) to the right of the vertical centre crease. Stencil with pale flesh pink paint. ▼

2 Clean and dry the stencil and flip it. Position the cutout on the lengthwise crease to the right of the first cherub with the elbows 2in (5cm) apart. Stencil the head and the arms as in step 1 (above).

3 Repeat steps 1-2 to stencil two cherubs to the left of the centre crease; the first one's head tilts to the right, the second one's head tilts to the left. Remove the masking tape, clean and dry the stencil and brush.

4 Mask off the head and the arm cutouts to reveal just the wings. Then realign the stencil over each cherub and stencil the wings in pale blue paint, flipping the stencil as necessary. ▼

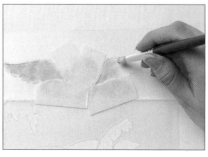

5 Clean and dry the stencil and brush. Position the hair cutout on each cherub and stencil the hair in golden yellow paint, flipping the stencil where necessary. Leave the paint to dry and fix it with a hot iron. ▼

6 Trace the face, wing and hair details from the picture (right) on to tracing paper. Transfer them on to each cherub using the dressmaker's carbon paper. Flip the tracing as necessary.

COLOUR KEY

COLOURS	SKEINS
335 Rose	1
798 Mid French blue	1
931 Metal blue	1
932 Mid metal blue	1
948 Peach-cream	1
3032 Manilla-beige	1
3753 Pale antique blue	1
3779 Pale rose-beige	1
3821 Old gold-yellow	1
5282 Metallic gold	1

PAINT COLOUR GUIDE

For the bodies: mix White with a tiny touch of Velvet Brown to make pale flesh pink.

For the wings: mix White with a little Cornflower to make pale blue.

For the hair: mix White with a touch of Fawn to make golden yellow.

EMBROIDERING THE CHERUBS

Refer to the stitch details (below) and use the embroidery hoop, moving the fabric along as you work. For the facial features, use one strand of stranded cotton (floss). Use one strand of stranded cotton (floss) and a strand of metallic gold together to stem stitch the hair, face, arms and the wings.

Making up the quilt

Take ⅝in (1.5cm) seam allowances throughout. Cut a 29 x 26¾in (73 x 68cm) rectangle of white fabric. Press the ribbon in half lengthwise. Tack it to the right side of the rectangle with the folded edge ¾in (2cm) from one short edge. With the raw edges matching and the right sides together, pin the cherub panel to the ribbon-trimmed panel. Stitch then press the seam towards the cherub panel. Cut 35 x 26¾in (89 x 68cm) of white fabric for the back. Place the front and back right sides together with the wadding (batting) on top. Stitch all around, leaving a 8in (20cm) gap at the bottom edge. Turn through to the right side and slipstitch the opening closed.

Use 798 to satin stitch the eyes, and 3032 to stem stitch the eyebrows and lids.

Outline the wings using a strand of gold with a strand of 3753 on the upper edges.

In the middle of the wing use gold and 932; on the lower edge use gold and 931.

Use gold with 3821 and 3032 for the hair.

Straight stitch in two strands of 3779 on the jawline and arms.

Straight stitch the nostrils in 3032, and the mouth in 335.

Use a strand each of gold and 948 on the upper edges of the arms; use gold and 3779 for the lower edges.

CHERUB CRIB DRAPE

The drape is made of 118in (300cm) wide Georgina fabric, the length of the drape support plus 4in (10cm). You will need all the stencilling and embroidery equipment and materials on page 10, plus spray mount and a water-soluble fabric marker.

Preparing the stencil

You will be using the flying cherub and his hair, shown in colour. Mask off any cutouts close to the one you are using. Spray mount the stencil.

Preparing the fabric

Fold fabric in half, selvedges together, and crease it. Mark cherub positions 4in (10cm) from right-hand raw edge, 9in (23cm) apart. Turn fabric over and repeat, but measure from left-hand edge. Unfold; lay out with a selvedge at the bottom and marks to the right.

Shell-stitched edging

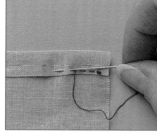
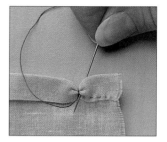

1 Fold a double hem. With the hem at the top, secure the thread at the right-hand edge. Work tiny running stitches over a distance of ⅜in (1cm) to the left, through all three layers of fabric.

2 Work two vertical stitches on top of each other, over the folded edge, pulling the thread tight to pinch the hem into a shell shape. Bring the needle through to the wrong side, ready to work running stitch again.

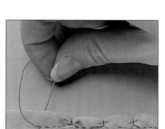

3 Continue in this way along the hem, alternating running stitches over ⅜in (1cm) of fabric, and a single vertical overcast stitch to form the shell edge.

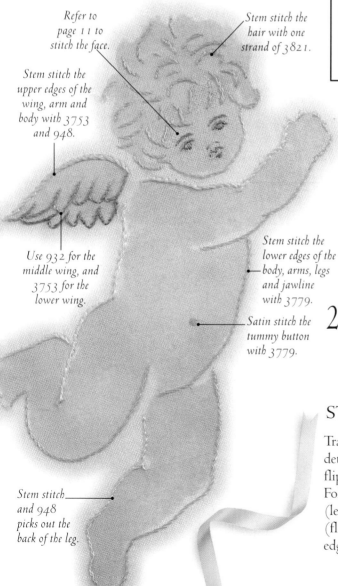

Refer to page 11 to stitch the face.

Stem stitch the hair with one strand of 3821.

Stem stitch the upper edges of the wing, arm and body with 3753 and 948.

Use 932 for the middle wing, and 3753 for the lower wing.

Stem stitch the lower edges of the body, arms, legs and jawline with 3779.

Satin stitch the tummy button with 3779.

Stem stitch and 948 picks out the back of the leg.

STENCILLING THE CHERUBS

1 Mask off wings. Position the cherub facing right with the hand on the first mark *below* the crease. Stencil it in pale flesh pink. Repeat at each mark *below* the crease. Clean the stencil and brush.

2 Stencil the hair in golden yellow. Unmask the wings and clean and dry the stencil and brush. Realign cutout; stencil the wings in pale blue.

3 Clean and dry the stencil and the brush. Spray mount the other side of the stencil and allow it to dry. Turn the fabric around so that the other selvedge is at the bottom and the marked edge is to the left.

4 Flip the stencil and repeat steps **1-2** to stencil four cherubs facing to the left. Allow the paints to dry and fix them with a hot iron.

STITCHING THE DRAPE

Trace the face, wing and hair details (left) and transfer them, flipping the tracing as necessary. Following the stitch details (left), use two strands of cotton (floss) to embroider the upper edges of the wing, arm and body.

Use one strand for the other details. To complete the drape, work a shell-stitched edging on the leading edge (see above). Stitch the back edges right sides together, trim and press the seam; turn to the right side.

Macdonald's Farm

A FAVOURITE RHYME COMES TO LIFE IN A NURSERY
NEAR YOU AS CUTE FARM ANIMALS MOO, OINK AND
BAA THEIR WAY INTO YOUR BABY'S HEART.

FARM WINDOW

A queue of friendly cows, pigs and sheep decorates a curtain border and tieback.

Preparing the fabric

For the curtain border: cut a strip of calico 5¼in (13.5cm) deep by the width of the curtain plus 1¼in (3cm) for turnings.

For the curtain tieback: cut a 21 x 5¼in (54 x 13.5cm) strip from the calico and one from the chambray.

Calico strips only: press a crease 1¼in (3cm) from each long edge. Lay them out flat.

To make soft piping: place a length of knitting yarn down the centre of the wrong side of a bias strip. Fold the strip over the yarn, matching the raw edges, and pin in place. Using a zipper foot, machine stitch close to the yarn with matching thread.

Preparing the stencil

The diagrams (right) show the farm animals stencil and the block border stencil. You need all the cutouts. Mask off any other nearby cutouts, then spray mount the back of the stencils and allow them to dry.

For the eyes and nostrils, use grey and move the needle around on the same spot.

Add detail to the clumps of grass with green thread.

Work double rows of grey straight stitch to outline the bodies and heads, and to create the tails.

STENCILLING THE BORDER AND TIEBACK

1 Place the block border cutout at the left-hand end of each calico strip with the top of the blocks on the top foldline. Stencil with mid blue. Repeat along the length. Repeat to stencil the block border with the bottom of the blocks on the lower foldline. ▼

2 Position the animal cutouts with the grass clumps ⅜in (1cm) above the lower block border and the first clump of grass ¾in (2cm) from the left-hand end of the fabric. Stencil the grass with Transparent Light Green. Repeat along the length of the calico. ▼

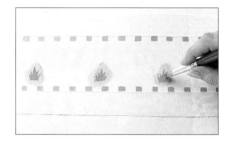

3 Stencil the animals' bodies referring to the paint colour guide (right) for colours, with a slightly mottled paint effect on the cow and pig. ▲

4 Stencil another group of animals 1in (2.5cm) to the right, then repeat across the calico strip. Finish with a clump of grass.

5 For the pigs' heads and the cows' heads and udders, lighten the mid pink and soft brown with White; use mid grey for the sheep's head. Stencil the heads and the cows' udders. Allow the paint to dry and fix it with a hot iron. ▲

COLOUR KEY

COLOURS	REELS
1041 Grey	1
1169 Green	1

PAINT COLOUR GUIDE

For the block border: mix White with a little Cornflower to make mid blue.

For the grass: use Transparent Light Green.

For the pigs: mix White with a little Bengal Pink to make mid pink.

For the cows: mix White with a little Velvet Brown to make soft brown.

For the sheep: use White for the bodies, and mix a little Mouse Grey with White to make mid grey for the faces.

STITCHING THE BORDER AND TIEBACK

Machine embroider the borders (details below).

Turn in and press ⅝in (1.5m) all around the curtain border then pin it across the curtain, 3¼in (8cm) above the bottom. Machine stitch close to the edge all around.

Press in ⅝in (1.5cm) all around the tieback and insert the pelmet interfacing. Press in ⅝in (1.5cm) all around the chambray strip. Slipstitch it to the tieback with the wrong sides together, inserting soft blue chambray piping all around. To finish, stitch a small brass ring to the back of the tieback at each end.

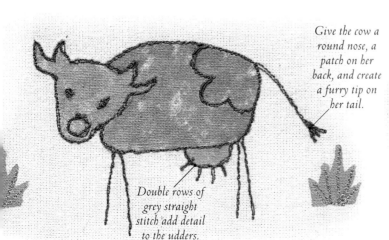

Give the cow a round nose, a patch on her back, and create a furry tip on her tail.

Double rows of grey straight stitch add detail to the udders.

Work double rows of grey in swirly shapes to suggest the sheep's woolly coat.

For the legs, use grey and a double row of straight stitch.

FARMYARD PICTURE

This cute farm animal appliqué is the perfect picture for a baby's room. For the background, use chambray left over from the tieback and use felt and fabric scraps for the animals and grass.

YOU WILL NEED

* Farm animal stencil
* Blue chambray, 9½in (24cm) square
* Scraps of felt in pink, beige and green
* Scraps of pink gingham, white fleece, and brown and grey wool fabrics
* DMC stranded cottons/ floss in ecru, 605 and 844
* Bondaweb/WonderUnder and pencil
* Picture frame with a 6¾ x 4¾in (17 x 12cm) aperture

WORKING THE APPLIQUE

1 Using the stencil cutouts as templates, draw each animal's body and head once only on to the paper side of the Bondaweb (WonderUnder), spacing them out. Draw the pig's snout and the cow's nose and udder, then draw six clumps of grass. Cut out the motifs roughly.

2 Bond the sheep's body to white fleece, and the head to grey wool. Bond the pig's body and snout to pink gingham and the head to pink felt. Bond the cow's body to brown wool and the head, udder and nose to beige felt. Bond the grass to green felt. Cut out the pieces accurately.

3 Bond the pig's body in the centre of the chambray, then bond the sheep 1in (2.5cm) above, and the cow 1in (2.5cm) below. Then bond the remaining pieces, with the clumps of grass at the sides. Use six strands of cotton (floss) for the embroidered details, as below, then frame the picture.

Use ecru to make French knots for the sheep's eyes and a tiny straight stitch for the mouth.

Using 844, make French knots for the pig's and cow's eyes and straight stitch their nostrils.

For the curly tail, couch down six strands of 605 with one strand of 605.

Straight s the cow's and its fur using 8.

Straight stitch the pig's legs with 605.

Use straight stitches and 844 for the cow's and sheep's legs and the udder details.

DUCK DELIGHT

FARMYARD DUCKS BOBBING ALONG THE RIVER
ARE A FAVOURITE CHILDHOOD IMAGE.
THEIR SIMPLE SHAPES ARE PERFECT
FOR EMBROIDERY.

QUILTED PLAYMAT

Proud mother ducks and fluffy ducklings swim sedately to and fro. Set these simple images on a softly padded fabric to create a playmat for a baby.

YOU WILL NEED

* 2yd (1.8m) of 36in (90cm) wide pale blue cotton fabric
* 1⅝yd (1.5m) of 36in (90cm) wide bright blue cotton fabric
* Mediumweight washable polyester wadding/ batting, 37½ x 33½in (95 x 85cm)
* Chalk and tape measure
* Lefranc et Bourgeois Textil Paint in White, Gold Yellow, Orange and France Blue
* Stencil and stencil brush
* White saucer
* Wallpaper lining paper and masking tape
* Tacking thread, sewing thread and needle
* DMC stranded cottons/floss as listed in the colour key

COLOUR KEY

COLOURS	SKEINS
■ 798 Blue	1
■ 971 Orange	1

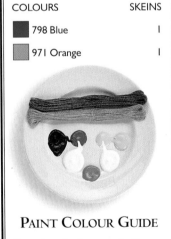

PAINT COLOUR GUIDE

For the ducks: mix half a pot of Gold Yellow with two drops of White to make yellow.

For the ripples: mix a drop of White with quarter pot of France Blue to make blue.

Three rows of bright yellow ducks swim in alternate directions across the mat. Their yellow bodies are stencilled first, then the orange beaks and eyes, and finally the watery blue ripples. The stencilled panel is framed with a bright blue border and padded with wadding (batting) to create a soft surface. The motifs are hand quilted in blue and orange to give the design a three-dimensional look. The mat measures 34¼ x 32¼in (87 x 82cm), and can also be used as a cosy pram or cot cover.

Preparing the stencil

The diagram (right) shows the complete stencil. For the playmat you will need all the motifs. You will be using the ducks first, so mask off the ripples, beaks and eyes before you start to stencil.

Preparing the fabric

Cut a 27¼ x 25¼in (69 x 64cm) piece of pale blue fabric. Chalk horizontal lines 7½in (19cm), 15in (38cm) and 23in (58cm) from the top of the fabric, and 2¾in (7cm) from the sides. Draw around the inside of the duck cutouts to mark their positions on the fabric, using the diagram above and the marked lines as a guide.

STENCILLING THE DESIGN

1 Stencil the top row of ducks first. Position the mother duck cutout on the markings and stencil her in yellow. Stencil the three baby ducks behind her in the same way. Repeat for the bottom row. Clean and dry the stencil, then flip it over to stencil the middle row with the ducks facing the other way.

2 Remove the masking tape, and clean the stencil and brush. Mask off any cutouts close to the beak and eye cutouts. Align the mother beak and eye cutouts over each mother duck and stencil in Orange. Stencil the baby beaks and eyes in the same way. Flip the stencil for the middle row. ➤

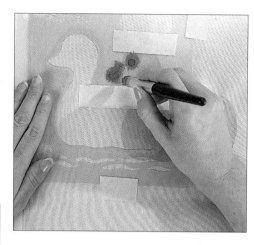

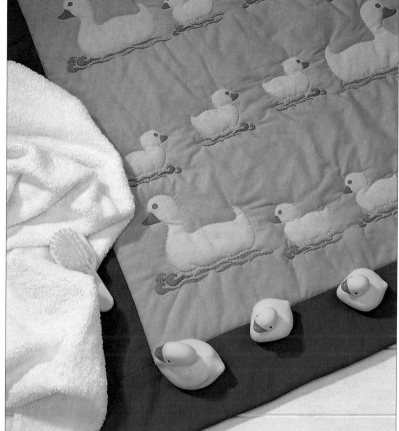

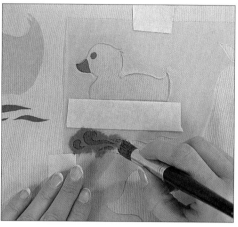

3 Clean and the dry the stencil and brush, then mask off the lower edges of the duck cutouts. Position the ripples cutout ¼in (6mm) below the first duck and stencil in blue. Repeat to stencil ripples below each duck, remembering to flip the stencil for the middle row. Allow the paint to dry, then fix it with a hot iron. ▲

STITCHING THE MAT

From pale blue fabric, cut one 35 x 33in (89 x 84cm) piece for the lining. *From bright blue fabric,* cut one 35 x 33in (89 x 84cm) piece for the backing, two 27¼ x 4¾in (69 x 12cm) border strips and two 33 x 4¾in (84 x 12cm) strips.

Taking ⅜in (1cm) seams, stitch the shorter border strips to the side edges of the stencilled panel, then stitch the longer border strips to the top and bottom edges. Press the seams open. Sandwich the wadding (batting) between the pale blue lining and the stencilled top, with the fabrics right sides out, and tack the layers together. Using two strands of orange cotton, hand quilt round the duck outlines. Hand quilt the ripples using two strands of blue. Remove the tacking.

Pin the bright blue backing to the mat, right sides together, and stitch all around, leaving a gap to turn through. Turn the mat right side out and slipstitch the opening closed. Machine stitch in the ditch created by the seam along the inner edges of the border, gently pulling the fabrics flat.

FLUFFY DUCKLING

Use the stencil as a template to cut a pattern for an adorable cuddly duckling. Made from fabric and felt with a polyester toy filling, it's the perfect gift for a baby.

YOU WILL NEED

* Short pile yellow fur fabric, 8in (20cm) square
* Orange felt
* Matching sewing threads
* Tracing paper and pencil
* Polyester toy filling

1 To make the patterns, trace the beak, eye and base templates (right) and cut them out. On the tracing paper, draw around the baby duck stencil. Omit the beak and straighten out the bottom edge. Draw another line ⅜in (1cm) outside the first. Cut out along the outer line. ▼

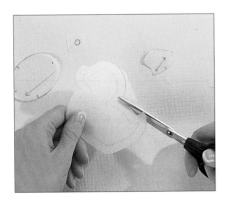

2 Pin the pattern pieces to the wrong side of the fur fabric and cut out. Flip the duck pattern and cut out again. From felt, cut out two beaks and two eyes.

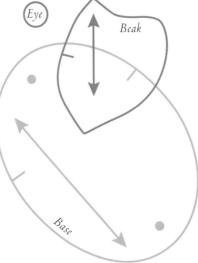

Eye

Beak

Base

3 Stitch the pieces right sides together, taking ⅜in (1cm) seams. Trim the seams and clip any curves. Start by stitching each beak to a duck. Next, stitch the duck pieces together, leaving the lower edge open and a 1in (2.5cm) gap in the back seam. Handstitch the base to the duck, then turn through to the right side. Stuff lightly, then slipstitch the gap closed. Handstitch the eyes in place.

BRIGHT IDEAS

POCKET APPLIQUE

Brighten up a child's bathrobe with a cheerful duck appliqué on the pocket. You'll need Bondaweb (WonderUnder), scraps of yellow fabric and orange felt for the beak. Using the baby duck stencil, follow the instructions on page 60 to appliqué the duck. Add an orange felt beak, then blanket stitch all around the edges with three strands of orange cotton (floss).

TEDDY BEARS

WITH THEIR PLUMP, FRIENDLY FIGURES AND SIMPLE
OUTLINES, TEDDY BEARS ARE IDEAL FOR NURSERY
APPLIQUES. USE YOUR STENCIL TO CREATE
ACCESSORIES TO WARM A BABY'S HEART.

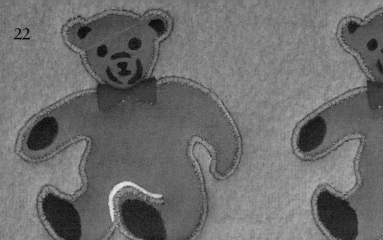

YOU WILL NEED

* ¾yd (60cm) of 64in (168cm) wide, pale blue polar fleece fabric
* ⅛yd (10cm) lightweight white cotton fabric
* Pebeo fabric paints in Raw Sienna, Chamois, and Vermilion
* Stencil and stencil brush
* White saucer
* Masking tape, kitchen paper and wallpaper lining paper
* Bondaweb/WonderUnder
* Threads to match fleece fabric and Raw Sienna paint
* DMC stranded cottons/floss as listed in the colour key
* Embroidery needle, size 6

COLOUR KEY

COLOURS	SKEINS
666 Scarlet	1
793 Slate blue	2

PAINT COLOUR GUIDE

For the teddy bears' bodies: use Raw Sienna.

For their faces and paws: use Chamois.

For their bow ties: use Vermilion.

MINI TEDDY BLANKET

A row of stencilled teddies, appliquéd on to a cosy polar fleece blanket, makes a friendly guard of honour for a baby's buggy.

This soft, warm blanket with its friendly teddy appliqués makes a cuddly, lightweight wrap for young babies and toddlers. The teddies are stencilled first on to white cotton — you can make up the blanket with its blanket stitched edge while the paint dries. The teddies are machine appliquéd on to the blanket, and their natty scarlet bow ties are hand embroidered. The finished blanket measures 28½ x 21in (72 x 54cm).

The friendly faces are stencilled in Chamois, and left as a paint effect.

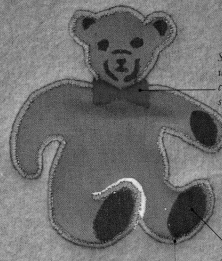

Satin stitch the bow ties using four strands of scarlet cotton (floss). Work the stitches vertically.

Machine stitch all round the teddies using an open zigzag and matching brown thread, then stitch round again with a close zigzag.

Like the faces, the ears, paws and feet are left as a paint effect.

Preparing the stencil

The diagram (right) shows the complete teddy bear stencil. For the blanket you need the two small bear cutouts, with the small paws, feet and face, shown in colour. While you are stencilling, mask off any cutouts close to the one you are using.

For smooth zigzag stitching round the curves of the teddies' bodies, stop every few stitches and pivot the fabric a little.

Large blanket stitches, worked in all six strands of slate blue cotton (floss), provide a decorative edging on the blanket.

STENCILLING THE TEDDY BEARS

1 The two small bears can be flipped to give four different bears. Stencil five small bears on to the white cotton fabric using Raw Sienna; flip the stencil for variety. Allow the paint to dry. ▲

2 Position the feet and paws and stencil them in Chamois paint. Position the small face cutout over the face and stencil the features, including the ears, in Chamois. Leave to dry. ▲

3 Reposition the bow tie where the chin and body meet and stencil it in Vermilion. Allow to dry and fix all the paints with a hot iron. ▲

STITCHING THE BLANKET

Cut two 29¾ x 22¼in (75 x 57cm) rectangles of polar fleece. Stitch them right sides together all around; take ⅝in (1.5cm) seam allowances and leave a gap to turn through. At the corners, snip diagonally across the seam allowances. Turn right sides out, and slipstitch the gap closed. Using six strands of 793 slate blue cotton (floss), blanket stitch all around the edges, making the stitches ⅝in (1.5cm) deep and ⅝in (1.5cm) apart.

Adding the teddies

Referring to page 60, fuse the Bondaweb (WonderUnder) on to the back of the stencilled teddies and cut them out. Fuse them in a row on the blanket, 2¾in (7cm) from the top edge. Machine zigzag stitch all around each teddy with matching brown thread. Using four strands of 666 scarlet, satin stitch the bow ties, working through the top layer of fabric only.

PADDED TEDDY BAG

YOU WILL NEED

- 1⅞yd (170cm) of 60in (150cm) wide blue cotton chambray
- 1⅛yd (1m) of 37¾in (96cm) wide washable polyester wadding/batting
- Washable polyester toy filling
- Washable felt in light brown, dark brown and red
- Stencil, stencil brush and masking tape
- Pebeo fabric paint in Chamois
- Air-erasable fabric marker
- Sewing threads to match chambray and felts
- Two black buttons, ⅜in (1cm) in diameter
- DMC stranded cottons/floss in black and 793
- Embroidery needle

A plump felt teddy makes an appealing motif on a nursery tote bag. The teddy is padded, and has shiny button eyes and a smart red waistcoat. The bag, made from chambray with a chambray lining, has a circular base and measures a generous 20in (51cm) deep.

Preparing the stencil

The diagram (left) shows the complete teddy stencil. For the bag you will be using the large teddy, and his paws, feet and waistcoat-front cutouts as templates. The face and ears are stencilled, so mask off any cutouts close to the face before stencilling.

Cutting out

From chambray: cut two 39 x 24¾in (99 x 63cm) rectangles for the bag sides; two 13¼in (33.5cm) diameter circles for the base; and two 35½ x 2⅛in (90 x 5.5cm) bias strips for the drawstring.

From wadding (batting): cut one 39 x 24¾in (99 x 63cm) rectangle; and one 13¼in (33.5cm) diameter circle. *From red felt:* cut out one waistcoat front, flip the stencil and repeat. *From dark brown felt:* cut two large paws and two large feet.

STITCHING THE TEDDY

Satin stitch the nose, working vertically.

The waistcoat buttons are French knots, worked with four strands of black cotton (floss)

1 On the light brown felt, use the air-erasable fabric marker to draw around the inside of the large teddy. Flip the stencil to complete the outline. Position the face and ears and stencil in Chamois paint. Allow to dry, then fix the paint with a hot iron.

2 Place one chambray rectangle with the shorter edges at the sides. Cut out the felt teddy and pin it centrally on the fabric, approximately 5¼in (13.5cm) above the lower edge. Oversew neatly all around with matching thread, leaving a 2in (5cm) gap. Stuff lightly with toy filling, using a pen to ease it into the paws and feet. Stitch the gap closed. ▶

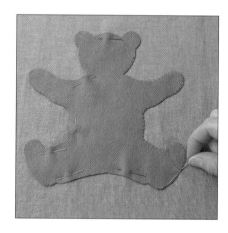

3 With matching threads, overstitch the waistcoat in place at shoulders and sides and slipstitch the paws and feet in place. Sew on the button eyes with four strands of 793 cotton (floss) and use four strands of black to satin stitch the nose and stem stitch the mouth.

MAKING UP THE BAG

Tack the wadding (batting) circle to the wrong side of one chambray circle, and the wadding (batting) rectangle to the wrong side of the chambray rectangle with the appliqué. Make up the bag as shown on page 59 using the unwadded (unbatted) chambray pieces for the lining. Stitch a ¾in (2cm) channel for the drawstring, 3¼in (8cm) below the top edge. To make the drawstring, join the two bias strips taking ¼in (6mm) seam allowances.

BIG CATS

MEET THE PUPPET STARS OF THE STITCH AND
STENCIL SHOW — TIGGER, THE TAMED AND STRIPY
TIGER, AND LEO, THE CUDDLY LION WITH THE
MAGNIFICENT WOOLLY MANE.

YOU WILL NEED

- ½yd (40cm) of mediumweight beige cotton fabric
- Matching sewing thread
- Pebeo fabric paint in Black
- Stencil and stencil brush
- Masking tape
- Kitchen paper and wallpaper lining paper
- Watercolour brush
- Tracing paper, two A3 sheets
- Pencil
- Water-soluble marker
- Dressmaker's carbon paper
- Scrap of pink felt
- Bondaweb/WonderUnder
- Polyester toy filling
- DMC stranded cottons/floss and tapestry wool as listed in the colour key
- Embroidery hoop
- Embroidery needle, size 7
- Scrap of card, 2in (5cm) wide

COLOUR KEY

COLOURS	SKEINS
Stranded cottons/floss	
310 Black	1
White	1
301 Mahogany	1
957 Mid geranium	1
Tapestry wool	
7505 Dark gold	3

LEO THE LION

 With his professional appearance and friendly lion smile, Leo the Lion is the king of the glove puppet jungle.

The trace-off pattern pieces for Leo and his friend Tigger are given on pages 78–9. The pieces are marked on the fabric before stencilling and stitching the face, and the paws are padded with felt and satin stitched. The woolly mane is worked in looped Turkey stitch after the puppet is made up.

Preparing the stencil
The diagram (right) shows the complete puppet stencil. For the lion, you will need the facial features only, shown here in colour; so mask off the stripes before you start.

MAKING PATTERNS

1 Fold the tracing paper sheets in half lengthwise. With the folds placed as indicated on the trace-off diagrams on the pattern, trace the body, back head and front head outlines, including the dots; cut them out and unfold to make patterns. Trace the ear outline and cut it out.

2 Pin the front head, back head and body patterns on the fabric. Draw round them, mark the dots, then unpin. Pin and draw round the body again; mark the dot. Draw round the ear pattern four times. Draw a 9 x 2¼in (23 x 5.5cm) bias strip for the tail.

Using three strands of cotton (floss) and working vertically, satin stitch the pupils in Black and the irises in Mahogany.

STENCILLING AND EMBROIDERING THE LION

1 Position the face cutout over the front head outline on the fabric. Stencil the eyes and nose in Black. Allow the paint to dry and fix it with a hot iron. ▼

2 On folded tracing paper, trace the mouth and the whisker dots from the pattern. Unfold the tracing and transfer it on to the front head using the dressmaker's carbon paper. ▼

3 Referring to the stitch details (below), use three strands of cotton (floss) to satin stitch the nose, pupils and the irises. Use four strands to backstitch the mouth and the eyelids. Use four strands for the French knots.

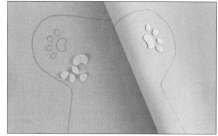

4 Trace the paw pads from the body diagram and transfer them twice on to the paper side of the Bondaweb (WonderUnder). Fuse this to the pink felt and cut out the pads, as on page 60. Referring to the diagram for positioning, fuse the pads in place on one body piece – this will be the front body. ▲

5 Using three strands of Mid geranium cotton, work satin stitch over the pink felt, referring to the stitch detail (left).

Single French knots, worked in three strands of White, add twinkles to Leo's eyes.

Use four strands of Black to backstitch the mouth and the inner edges of the eyelids.

Pick out the whisker dots with French knots, and four strands of Black.

Working vertically, satin stitch the nose with three strands of Black cotton (floss).

The plump paws are padded with felt, then satin stitched with four strands of Mid geranium.

MAKING UP LEO THE LION

Take ⅜in (1cm) seam allowances and stitch all the seams right sides
together. Snip any curves and corners and press the seam allowances open.

1 Cut out all the pieces along the marked lines. Pin and tack the bodies together leaving the lower edge open. Stitch then snip to the dots. On the lower edge, press under ⅜in (1cm) then 1in (2.5cm). Slipstitch the hem neatly. Turn the body through to the right side and press it. ➤

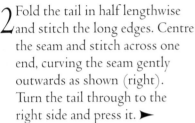

2 Fold the tail in half lengthwise and stitch the long edges. Centre the seam and stitch across one end, curving the seam gently outwards as shown (right). Turn the tail through to the right side and press it. ➤

3 Centre the open end of the tail at the back of the puppet on the lower edge and handstitch it in place, tucking in the raw edges.

4 Stitch the darts on the front head right sides together; match the two edges of each V shape, follow the dotted stitching lines on the pattern, and stop stitching at the dots. Clip the darts and press them open. ▼

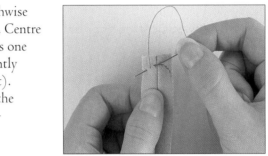

Work the mane and tail tuft in Turkey stitch, making the loops 2in (5cm) deep – use the 2in (5cm) wide scrap of card to check the size of each one.

Cut the loops with sharp scissors for a neat, blunt finish.

For a really dense mane, use a double thickness of tapestry wool.

If you want the tail tuft to be longer than the mane, work slightly deeper Turkey stitch loops.

5 Stitch the ears together in pairs leaving the lower edges open. Trim the seams, clip the curves and turn through to the right side. Pin and tack the ears to the front head between the dots. ▲

STITCHING THE LION'S MANE AND TAIL

Referring to the stitch detail (above), use a double length of tapestry wool to work Turkey stitch all around the head seam. Cut the loops and trim the mane neatly. Work the tuft on the end of the tail in the same way.

6 Stitch the front and back head pieces together, leaving the neck edge open between the dots. Snip to the dots, turn under the raw edges between the dots and tack them in place. Turn the head through to the right side. ▼

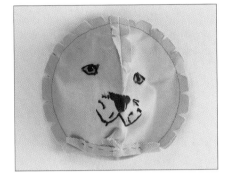

7 Stuff the head firmly with the polyester toy filling. Poke two fingers into the head to make a clearing in the middle. ▼

8 Slip your hand into the body, with one finger in the projection at the top. Place the head on top, facing forward. Pin and tack the head to the body. Slipstitch the head securely in place along the folded neck edge. ▼

TIGGER THE TIGER

Tigger is made up just like his puppet friend Leo the Lion, using apricot fabric instead of beige. You'll need all the other materials listed on page 26, except the tapestry wool.

Prepare the pattern pieces and transfer them to the fabric following the steps on page 27. To stencil and stitch the stripes, follow the steps overleaf and refer to the diagrams on the pattern for positioning.

Preparing the stencil

The diagram (right) shows the complete puppet stencil. For the tiger you will need all the cutouts – the facial features and the stripes. As you work, mask off any cutouts close to the one you are using.

STENCILLING THE TIGER

1 Mask off the single stripe cutout at the top left corner of the stencil. Position the face cutout over the front head outline on the fabric and stencil the eyes, nose and face stripes in Black. ▼

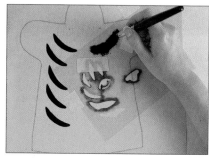

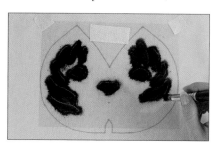

2 Unmask the single stripe cutout. On one half of the back head, stencil three stripes. Clean and flip the stencil and repeat on the other half. ▼

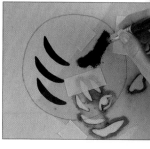

3 On one side of the body piece, use the single stripe cutout to stencil five stripes. Clean and flip the stencil, and stencil five stripes on the other side. Repeat to stencil the second body piece.

4 On the tail, draw lines ⅝in (1.5cm) apart. With these as guide lines, paint stripes with the watercolour brush. When all the paint is dry, fix it with a hot iron. ▼

Work the iris in Mahogany and the rest of the facial features in Black.

On the lower face, use a single strand of White to suggest the fur.

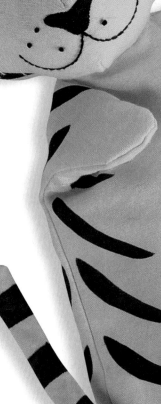

Single straight stitches in one strand of Mahogany, suggest fur on the upper face.

A single French knot in three strands of White adds a happy gleam to the tiger's eye.

STITCHING THE FUR

Embroider the facial features as for the lion on page 27. Then, referring to the details (right), use a single strand of Mahogany cotton (floss) to work straight stitches to suggest fur on the back head and the upper part of the front head. On the front head, use a single strand of White to work straight stitches on the lower stripes.

Work the paw pads and make up the tiger in the same way as the lion, referring to pages 27–9.

SNAKES AND LADDERS

REVISIT HAPPY CHILDHOOD MEMORIES
WITH A BRIGHT FELT VERSION
OF THE WELL-LOVED
BOARD GAME.

YOU WILL NEED

- ❋ Blue felt, two 20½in (52cm) squares
- ❋ Felt squares in shocking pink, green, yellow and orange
- ❋ Snakes and ladders stencil
- ❋ Stencil brush
- ❋ Pebeo fabric paint in Velvet Brown
- ❋ Masking tape and spray mount
- ❋ Kitchen paper and wallpaper lining paper
- ❋ Ruler and air-erasable fabric marker
- ❋ Bondaweb/WonderUnder and sharp HB pencil
- ❋ Dark royal blue button thread
- ❋ Dark royal blue machine thread (optional)
- ❋ Matching sewing threads
- ❋ 2¾yd (2.5m) of 1in (2.5cm) wide dark blue bias binding

GAME MAT

Count the squares, climb the ladders, slip down the snakes — but be the first to reach the finish.

The mat is made of felt, with a grid of bold machine stitching to mark the squares. The ladders are stencilled at rakish angles, and the wiggly snakes and the directional arrows are appliquéd in brightly coloured felts. The numerals are embroidered in simple stitches and the snakes' creepy eyes are satin stitched for added texture and detail. The mat is then backed with another layer of felt, finished with bias binding and when complete, measures 20½in (52cm) square. To make the giant dice and counters, turn to page 34.

Preparing the stencil

The diagram (right) shows the complete snakes and ladders stencil. You will be stencilling the ladders first so mask off any nearby cutouts. The snakes and arrow are used as templates for appliqué. Spray mount the back of the stencil before you start and leave it to dry.

Preparing the game mat

Use the air-erasable fabric marker to draw a line 2¼in (6cm) from each edge. Mark the inner square at 2in (5cm) intervals on each side. Join opposite marks, extending the lines to the edges of the felt, to give a grid of 100 squares. With button thread in the needle, machine straight stitch the lines. If your machine does not take button thread, work a double row of ordinary machine thread.

STENCILLING THE LADDERS

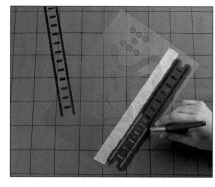

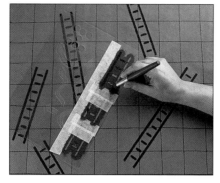

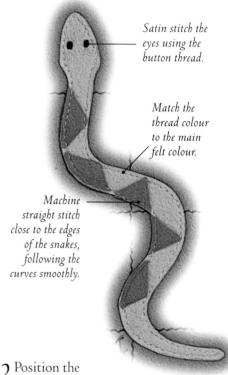

1 Place the ladder cutout at an angle on the mat, with the base and tip centred in squares. Stencil with Velvet Brown. Reposition, tilting the ladder in the opposite direction, and stencil it again. ▲

2 Mask the ladder to give an eight-rung ladder. Stencil it three times at different angles. Remask to give a four-rung ladder and stencil it three times. Allow the paint to dry and fix it with a warm iron. ▲

Satin stitch the eyes using the button thread.

Match the thread colour to the main felt colour.

Machine straight stitch close to the edges of the snakes, following the curves smoothly.

MAKING THE GAME MAT

1 On the paper side of the Bondaweb (WonderUnder), use the cutouts as templates to draw four large, four medium and three small snakes; flip the stencil for variety. Draw ten arrows, then draw a 1¼in (3cm) diameter circle.

2 Cut out the motifs roughly. Bond the snakes to the different coloured felt squares, and bond the arrows and the circle to the pink felt. Cut out all the pieces accurately. For details, see page 60.

3 Position the snakes on the game mat with the heads and tails centred in squares; place some across the ladders. Bond them in place as on page 60.

4 Lay the snake cutouts on the paper side of the Bondaweb (WonderUnder), and draw stripes and triangles inside them. Cut them out roughly and bond them to contrasting coloured felts. Cut out the shapes accurately and bond them in place on the snakes. ▼

5 Position one of the arrows on the felt in the bottom left-hand square and bond it in place. Position the remaining arrows in the squares at alternate ends of each row. Centre the pink circle in the top left-hand square and bond it in place. ▼

6 Use matching threads to machine stitch around the edges of the snakes, the arrows and the circle. Using the buttonhole thread and straight and fly stitches, work ⅜in (1cm) high numbers in the squares. Satin stitch the snakes' eyes.

7 Place the second felt square behind the stitched piece, then bind the edges together with navy blue bias binding.

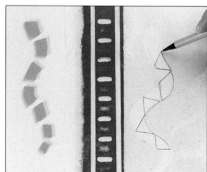

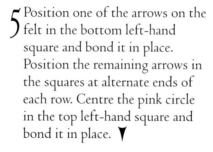

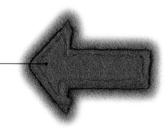

Pink felt arrows indicate the starting point and the direction of play.

Create felt stripes for some of the snakes. On other snakes, a row of triangles imitates snakeskin patterns.

DICE AND COUNTERS

Preparing the stencil

The diagram (right) shows the complete snakes and ladders stencil. You will be using the dice cutouts so mask off any other nearby cutouts, then mask off the dots as you work.

Leave the stencilled dots as a paint effect.

MAKING THE DICE

1 For each dice cut six 2¾in (72mm) squares of one felt colour. Referring to the diagram (left), use Cobalt Blue to stencil the appropriate number of dots on each felt square, masking off the stencil as necessary. Allow the paint to dry and fix it with a hot iron. ▲

2 With ¼in (6mm) seams, stitch the squares together as shown in the diagram (left); start and finish ¼in (6mm) from the ends of each seam. Stitch the joined squares to form a cube, leaving one side open. Stuff the cube with the toy filling then slipstitch the last side.

MAKING COUNTERS

For each counter, use the air-erasable fabric marker to draw a 1¼in (3cm) diameter circle on felt. Pin a slightly smaller circle of wadding (batting) behind it. Pin another layer of felt underneath and machine straight stitch along the drawn circle. Cut out just outside the stitching. ▼

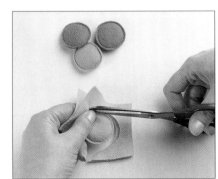

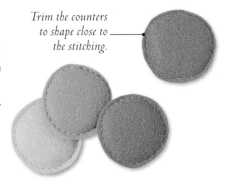

Trim the counters to shape close to the stitching.

CUDDLY SHEEP

FOR PEACEFUL BEDTIMES AND QUIET NIGHTS,
STENCIL, APPLIQUE AND EMBROIDER SHEEP
ON SOFT BEDROOM
ACCESSORIES.

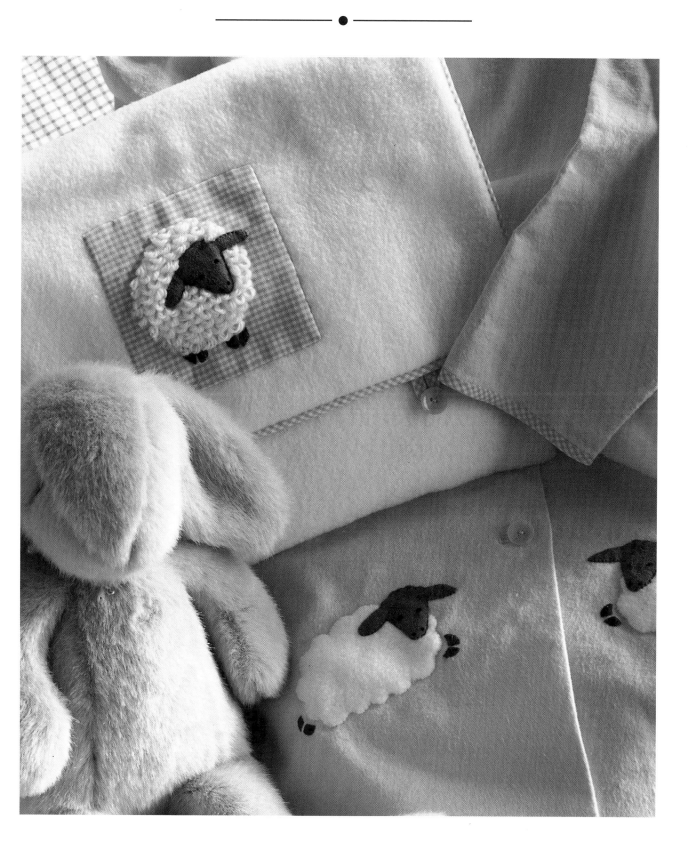

NIGHTDRESS CASE

A soft and cuddly nightdress case, its contents watched over by a friendly woolly sheep, is the perfect accessory for a little girl's bedroom.

The case is made from creamy polar fleece fabric and lined with warm pink brushed cotton to match the nightshirt (see overleaf). The sheep is stencilled on a gingham patch, and its woolly coat is worked in Turkey stitch and tapestry wool to make a thick looped pile. The finished sheep patch is appliquéd on to the front of the nightdress case, which is trimmed with matching pink gingham piping.

The finished nightdress case measures 13½ x 11½in (34 x 29cm) with a straight-edged, 8in (20cm) deep flap. For information on pile stitches, see page 65.

Preparing the stencil
The diagram (right) shows the sheep stencil. For the case you will be using the oval sheep's body as a stencil, and the head, eyes and nose and feet as templates to draw around. Before you start, mask off any cutouts close to the body.

WORKING THE SHEEP PATCH

1 Cut a piece of pink gingham 5¼in (13cm) square. In the centre, stencil the oval sheep's body in White. Allow to dry and fix with a hot iron. Position the feet cutouts below the body and draw around them with the fabric marker. ▼

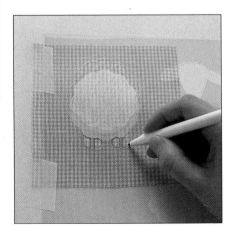

2 On the grey felt, draw around the inside of the head cutout. Position the eyes and nose on the drawn face and mark their positions. Cut out the head. ▲

Tilt the head to give the sheep a whimsical look, and slipstitch it in place with tiny, neat stitches.

STITCHING THE SHEEP

Using three strands of dark grey cotton (floss) and the embroidery needle, satin stitch the feet. Use the chenille needle and white tapestry wool to fill in the body with Turkey stitch, leaving the loops uncut. Slipstitch the head in place with grey thread. Use the embroidery needle to satin stitch the eyes and nose with three strands of black cotton (floss).

To make the piping

Measure round the piping cord and add 1¼in (3cm). Cut a strip of gingham to this width, wrap it around the cord matching raw edges and machine stitch close to the cord using a zipper foot.

Uncut Turkey stitch, worked in dense rows, represents the sheep's woolly coat.

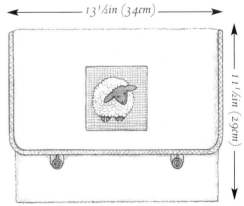

— 13½in (34cm) —

8in (20cm)

11½in (29cm)

Making up

Make up the nightdress case to the measurements shown (above); follow the instructions on pages 57–8, adding the gingham piping and button loops at step **3**. Turn in ⅝in (1.5cm) all around the sheep patch and slipstitch it on to the flap. Add the buttons.

LEAPING SHEEP

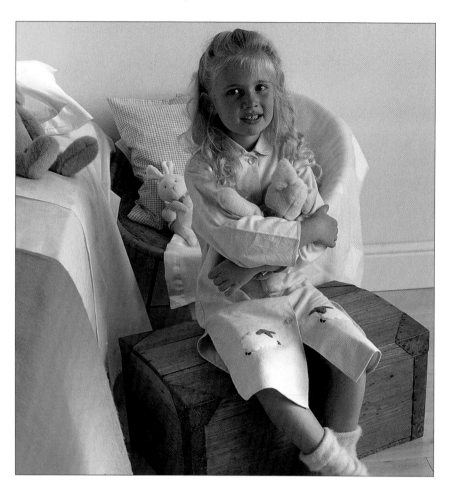

Ready for the count-down to sleep, fluffy sheep gambol around a soft nightshirt. Appliquéd in fleece fabric and grey felt, they are shown here on a brushed cotton nightshirt. Try this idea on ready-made nightwear.

YOU WILL NEED

- ✳ Nightshirt
- ✳ Scraps of cream polar fleece fabric
- ✳ Washable grey felt
- ✳ Sheep stencil
- ✳ DMC stranded cottons/floss as listed on page 36
- ✳ Fabric marker
- ✳ Sewing needle and white and grey sewing threads
- ✳ Embroidery needle, size 8

Using the stencil

The diagram (below) shows the complete sheep stencil. For the nightshirt, you will need the feet, the head, the face and the sideways-facing body.

Satin stitch the eyes and nose.

Use tiny slipstitches to appliqué the body and head.

STITCHING

1 On the polar fleece, draw around the inside of the sideways-facing body cutout as many times as required, and cut out. On the grey felt, draw the same number of heads. Position the eyes and nose cutouts on each face and mark their positions, then cut out the heads.

2 Slipstitch the bodies on to the nightshirt, placing them at different angles so that they look as though they are leaping. Slipstitch the heads in position with grey sewing thread.

3 Position the feet cutouts and draw them on to the garment with the fabric marker. Using three strands of cotton (floss), satin stitch the feet in dark grey and the eyes and nose in black.

BRIGHT IDEAS

SHEEP POCKET

Carry the sheep theme on to a dressing gown pocket. On a square of pink fabric, stencil the sheep's body in white paint, then the head and feet in grey paint. Allow to dry and fix with a hot iron. Satin stitch the feet in grey and the eyes and nose in black using three strands of cotton (floss). If you want a quilted effect, machine stitch round the body and head. Turn in the edges of the patch and stitch it to the pocket.

RABBIT SLIPPERS

ENCHANTING RABBIT TWINS
WILL BE FAVOURITE COSY INDOOR
FOOTWEAR FOR A YOUNG
CHILD.

YOU WILL NEED

- ❀ ¼yd (20cm) of 36in (90cm) wide pale grey felt
- ❀ ¼yd (20cm) of 36in (90cm) wide pink felt
- ❀ Rabbit slippers stencil
- ❀ Stencil brush
- ❀ Pebeo fabric paint in White and Bengal Pink
- ❀ Masking tape
- ❀ White saucer, kitchen paper and wallpaper lining paper
- ❀ Tracing paper and pencil
- ❀ Dressmaker's carbon paper
- ❀ Fabric marker
- ❀ DMC stranded cottons/floss as listed in the colour key
- ❀ Mediumweight polyester wadding/batting, 8in (20cm) square
- ❀ Pink and grey sewing threads
- ❀ Embroidery needle, size 7
- ❀ 4in (10cm) of 36in (90cm) wide pelmet sew-in interfacing
- ❀ Bodkin and 6¾in (17cm) of 5/16in (8mm) wide elastic
- ❀ Fabric glue
- ❀ DMC tapestry wool, two skeins of white
- ❀ Stiff card, 8 x 4in (20 x 10cm)
- ❀ Pair of compasses

COLOUR KEY

COLOURS		SKEINS
☐ White		1
■ 310 Black		1
■ 317 Mid pewter		1

PAINT COLOUR GUIDE

Mix White with a dash of Bengal Pink to make a shade of pink to match the pink felt.

MAKING THE SLIPPERS

Simple stencilled and stitched faces, cute bunny ears and fluffy pompon tails turn plain slippers into a pair of adorable little rabbits.

The slippers are made from felt, available by the yard (metre) from mail order suppliers in a range of colours. Ideally, use washable felt. The ones shown here are made in pink and grey, but you could use brown and cream or any combination of colours you prefer. The rabbit stencil gives the cutouts for the face and the inner ears.

Preparing the stencil

The diagram (below) shows the rabbit stencil. You will be using all the cutouts. Mask off any other nearby cutouts before you start.

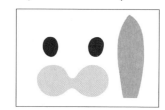

STENCILLING THE FACES AND EARS

1 Trace the sole, and front and back upper patterns from the pattern on page 80; for more details, refer to pages 55–6. Cut out the tracings to make patterns.

2 On the pale grey felt, use the fabric marker to draw around the front upper pattern twice. Then draw around the back upper pattern twice.

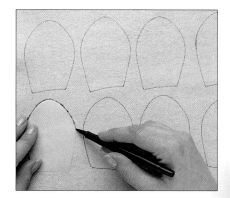

3 On the pale grey felt again, draw around the ear pattern four times – these are the four right-hand ears. Flip the pattern and draw around it four more times to mark the four left-hand ears. ▲

4 On the pink felt, draw around the front and back upper patterns twice. Then draw around the sole pattern four times on the pink felt.

5 On the stencil, mask off the inner ear cutout. Centre the muzzle and eyes cutout on one marked pale grey front upper and stencil it with pink paint. Repeat to stencil the muzzle on the second pale grey front upper. ▲

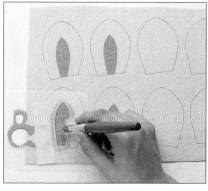

6 Centre the inner ear cutout on two left ears, as shown. Stencil in Pink. Clean, dry and flip the stencil. Reposition on two right ears and stencil again. When dry, fix the paint with a hot iron. ▲

EMBROIDERING

Trace off the nose, mouth, teeth and whiskers from the picture (below). Place the tracing over the stencilled muzzle and transfer the outlines with the dressmaker's carbon paper.

Embroider the face referring to the details (below) for stitch directions. Use three strands of black cotton (floss) to satin stitch the eyes and the nose, and stem stitch the mouth. Use three strands of white cotton (floss) to satin stitch the teeth, then use two strands of Mid pewter to stem stitch the whiskers.

For the bobtails, stitch a small white pompon to the back of each slipper.

Satin stitch each eye in Black, working vertically. A French knot, worked with three strands of White, adds a cheeky twinkle.

Stem stitch the whiskers with two strands of Mid pewter.

Use Black to satin stitch the nose, working vertically.

Stem stitch the mouth in Black.

Work the teeth with horizontal satin stitches using white cotton (floss).

MAKING THE SLIPPERS

1 Cut out all the felt pieces along the drawn lines, then use the ear pattern to cut four ear pieces from the wadding (batting).

2 Place a wadding (batting) ear to the wrong side of each stencilled ear. Place each wadded (batted) ear on a plain ear with the felt sides together. Tack the layers together all around. Stitch, taking ¼in (6mm) seam allowances and leaving the straight lower edges of the ears open to turn through.

6 Make the slippers, sandwiching the ears between the stencilled and the plain front uppers. For details, see pages 55–6.

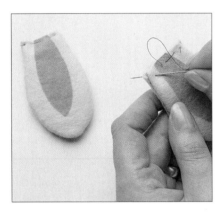

3 Turn the ears through to the right side and tack across the lower edges. ▲

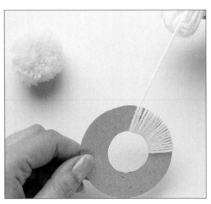

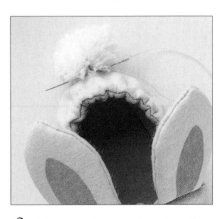

7 Cut two 2¾in (7cm) diameter card circles with a 1¼in (3cm) diameter centre hole. Wind the tapestry wool round the card until the ring is full. Cut around the outer edges, tie tightly around the middle leaving the yarn long, remove the card and fluff out the pompon. ▲

8 Using matching sewing thread and the sewing needle, stitch one pompon firmly to the centre back of each slipper. ▲

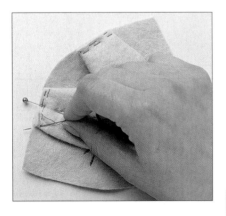

4 Position an ear on one of the stencilled front uppers, positioning it between two of the dots: make sure that the stencilled side of the ear faces down. Tack the ear in place with the raw edges level, then repeat with a second ear. ▲

5 Tack the remaining ears on to the second stencilled front upper; make sure the left and right-hand ears are correctly placed.

BRIGHT IDEAS

RABBIT POCKET

Copy the rabbit slippers idea to make a fun dressing-gown pocket. Cut a pale grey felt pocket and stencil and stitch the face, as on page 41. Make a pair of ears, as on pages 41–2. Cut a pink felt lining to match the pocket. Slip the ears between the top of the pocket and the lining, and topstitch along the top edge. Stitch the pocket in place on the dressing gown.

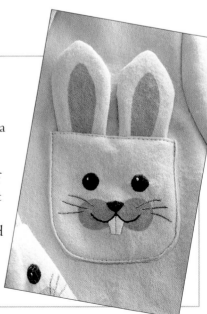

FELT TRINKETS

USE BRIGHT FELTS, SHINY THREADS, FUN BEADS
AND SWEET STENCILLED MOTIFS
TO MAKE FUN TRINKETS
IN A TRICE.

FRIENDSHIP BRACELETS

Quick to make and fun to wear, a felt friendship bracelet makes a perfect small gift.

A fashion favourite with young girls, these inexpensive friendship bracelets are easy enough for a child to make. Use felt squares, available from mail order craft suppliers in an extensive range of vibrant colours. Choose your own combinations or copy the colour schemes shown on these pages.

The designs are stencilled on to the upper felt strip and then beads and embroidery stitches are added to decorate and hold the layers together. The plaited ties are made from glossy rayon threads for extra colour detail.

Preparing the stencil

The diagram (right) shows the complete bracelet stencil. For each bracelet, you will be using one of the rows of motifs shown in colour.

Before you start, mask off any nearby cutouts. Lightly spray mount the back of the stencil and leave it to dry.

Cutting out

For each bracelet, choose two felt colours. On one, draw a 6 x 1¼in (15 x 3cm) strip; on the other draw a 5½ x ¾in (14.5 x 2cm) strip. Cut them out on the drawn lines with scissors or pinking shears. Use the drawn side as the wrong side.

STENCILLING THE BRACELETS

Centre the chosen cutouts on the smaller felt strip and stencil with the chosen paint colour, straight from the pot. Allow the paint to dry and fix it with a hot iron. ▼

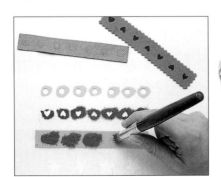

YOU WILL NEED

❋ Craft felt in bright colours, 8½in (22cm) square of each
❋ Bracelet stencil and stencil brush
❋ Pebeo fabric paints in Opaque Buttercup Yellow, Opaque Cherry Red, Parma Violet and Opaque Bengal Pink
❋ Masking tape
❋ Spray mount
❋ Kitchen paper and wallpaper lining paper
❋ Metallic seed beads and larger glass beads
❋ DMC rayon threads as listed in the colour key
❋ Embroidery needle, size 8
❋ Sharp scissors and pinking shears
❋ Hole punch

COLOUR KEY

COLOURS	SKEINS
30471 Pale avocado	1
30552 Mid violet	1
30554 Pale violet	1
30601 Dark pink	1
30606 Orange	1
30666 Flame red	1
30973 Canary yellow	1
30996 Mid turquoise	1

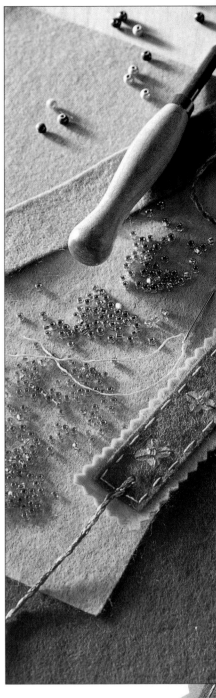

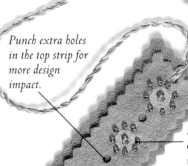

Decorate the flowers with straight and slanted cross stitches and a seed bead at the centre.

Punch extra holes in the top strip for more design impact.

Make of see round circle, anoth at the

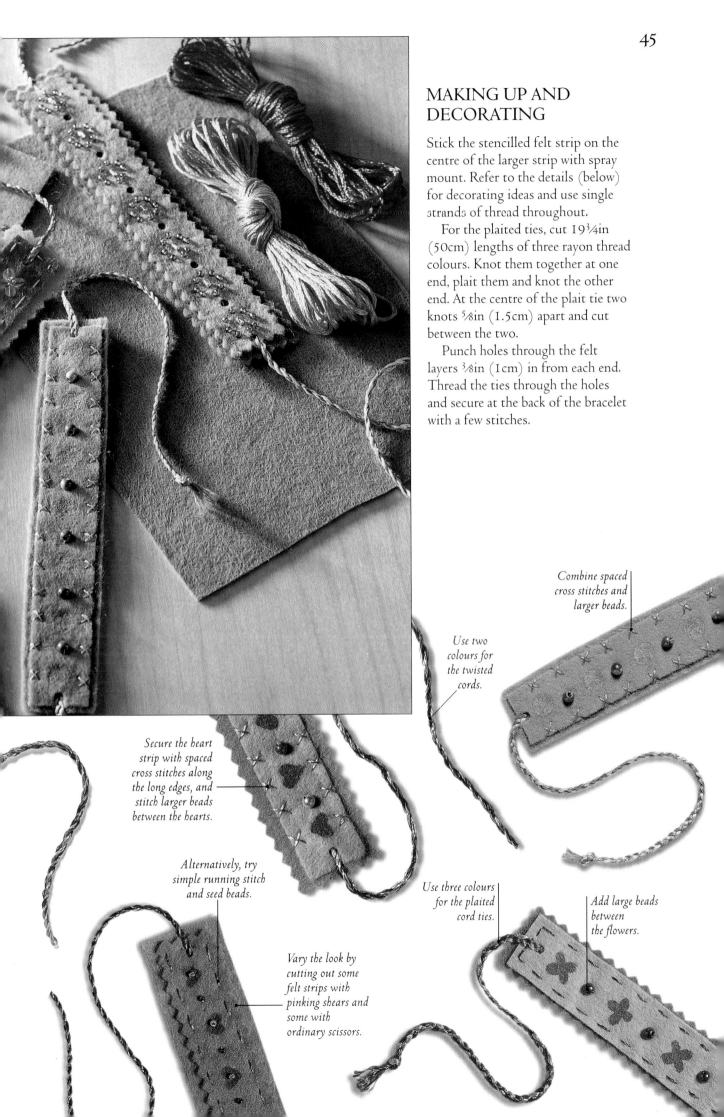

MAKING UP AND DECORATING

Stick the stencilled felt strip on the centre of the larger strip with spray mount. Refer to the details (below) for decorating ideas and use single strands of thread throughout.

For the plaited ties, cut 19¾in (50cm) lengths of three rayon thread colours. Knot them together at one end, plait them and knot the other end. At the centre of the plait tie two knots ⅝in (1.5cm) apart and cut between the two.

Punch holes through the felt layers ⅜in (1cm) in from each end. Thread the ties through the holes and secure at the back of the bracelet with a few stitches.

Combine spaced cross stitches and larger beads.

Use two colours for the twisted cords.

Secure the heart strip with spaced cross stitches along the long edges, and stitch larger beads between the hearts.

Alternatively, try simple running stitch and seed beads.

Use three colours for the plaited cord ties.

Add large beads between the flowers.

Vary the look by cutting out some felt strips with pinking shears and some with ordinary scissors.

FELT CHOKERS

These eyecatching chokers are worked on subtle felts in grey and beige with stars stencilled in Pearl Light Copper paint, shiny sequins and beads and easy stitching in glossy rayon threads.

YOU WILL NEED

❋ Felt in beige and silver-grey, 8½in (22cm) square of each

❋ Star bracelet stencil and stencil brush

❋ Pebeo fabric paint in Pearl Light Copper

❋ DMC rayon threads as listed in the colour key

❋ Dark gold sequins

❋ Seed beads in gold and copper

❋ Embroidery needle, size 8

COLOUR KEY

COLOURS	SKEINS
■ 30301 Mahogany	1
▨ 30415 Pearl grey	1
▦ 30841 Coffee	1

STENCILLING

For each choker, draw a 1⅜in (3.5cm) strip diagonally across each felt square. Cut out with scissors or pinking shears; leave the point if desired. Stencil seven stars on either the beige or grey felt strip.

MAKING UP

Use scissors or pinking shears to cut the star strip into squares. Stick to the second strip with spray mount.

Secure the pinked squares with seed beads at the corners and at the centre of each star. Work a cross stitch in each corner of the plain squares with one strand of Mahogany; use a seed bead to secure a sequin at the centre of each star. Work running stitch around the choker using two strands of Mahogany.

Referring to page 45, punch two holes at the straight-cut ends and single holes at the pointed ends, and add plaited ties.

A SPECIAL GIFT

Make this sweetheart bracelet for a special friend.

Centre the row of heart cutouts on the beige felt. Draw around the inside of the motifs with a fine fibre-tipped pen.

Working vertically, satin stitch the hearts using one strand of red rayon thread.

Trim the edges of the red felt with pinking shears. Centre the stencilled and stitched beige felt strip on top. Using one strand of red thread, stitch two seed beads between each heart, stitching through all the layers.

For the ties, plait together three strands each of beige and red thread; for details on making and attaching them see page 45.

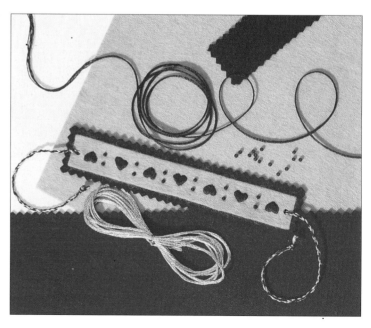

SAIL AWAY

LITTLE BOATS, SAILS BILLOWING IN THE WIND, SCUD ACROSS
A SEA OF CHOPPY WAVES. PERFECT FOR APPLIQUE,
THIS STITCH AND STENCIL DESIGN WILL APPEAL
TO BUDDING YOUNG SEAFARERS.

SAILING POCKET TIDY

Scraps of mini-check fabrics, appliquéd and
embroidered with simple straight stitches,
make charming pocket pictures for a wall tidy.

The sailing boats, waves and clouds
are appliquéd on to three denim
patches, secured with topstitching
and decorated with straight stitches.
The seagulls are stencilled in White
for textural contrast. The patches are
then stitched to a strip of hessian to
make pockets. The pocket tidy is
embellished with string and shells to
give it a maritime flourish.

You will need only small pieces of
fabric, so hunt through your box of
remnants. Choose lightweight mini-
print cotton fabrics that work well
together and show up against the
denim background. Make sure that
all the fabrics, including the denim,
are washed and pressed before use.
The finished wall hanging measures
27¼ x 11in (69 x 28cm).

Preparing the stencil
The diagram (right) shows
the complete boat stencil.
The large boat, cloud and
waves are used as templates
for the appliqué. The birds
are stencilled afterwards, so
there is no need to mask off
anything before you start.

YOU WILL NEED

❋ Three well-washed
 denim patches, each 7½in
 (19cm) square
❋ Hessian, 28¾ x 12½in
 (73 x 32cm)
❋ Pebeo fabric paint in
 White
❋ Masking tape
❋ Bondaweb/WonderUnder
❋ Pencil
❋ Scraps of plain cream and
 five mini-print fabrics
❋ Navy sewing thread
❋ DMC stranded
 cottons/floss as listed in
 the colour key
❋ Embroidery needle, size 8
❋ 2¼yd (2m) of garden
 string
❋ Four shells
❋ Dowelling, 11in (28cm)
 long (optional)

COLOUR KEY

COLOURS	SKEINS
☐ Ecru	1
■ 221 Rust	1
▨ 3778 Pink	1

WORKING THE APPLIQUE

1 On the paper side of the Bondaweb (WonderUnder), draw inside the cloud, waves, large boat hull, mast, sail and pennant cutouts. Repeat twice. Cut out roughly; bond to the wrong side of your chosen fabrics. Cut out the shapes accurately.

2 Bond the motifs on to the denim squares, as on page 60. Apply the cloud first, then the sail, so that it overlaps the cloud slightly. Allow the waves to overlap the bottom of the hull. Mask off any cutouts close to the seagulls and stencil them in White. ▼

STITCHING THE PATCHES

Using navy thread and a small straight stitch, machine stitch around the motifs, 1/16in (2mm) from the edges. With two strands of ecru cotton (floss), work vertical straight stitches at the base of the waves. With one strand of Rust, work single long straight stitches on each side of the masts and along the straight edges of the hulls. With two strands of Pink, work running stitches 1in (2.5cm) from the sides and base of each patch.

Making up the hanging

Turn in ¾in (2cm) along the side and base edges of the hessian and machine stitch in place with navy thread. Repeat to hem the top of the hessian, leaving the ends open.

Turn in ⅝in (1.5cm) all around each patch and press. Machine stitch the top edge only. Pin the pockets to the hessian strip and machine stitch around the sides and base.

Using all six strands of ecru cotton (floss), couch the string 1in (2.5cm) from the pockets. Attach a shell at each corner by stitching over it several times. If you wish to strengthen the top hem, thread the dowelling through it. Knot the ends of a 10in (25cm) piece of string; stitch it to the back of the hessian at the top to hang it.

DENIM BOAT PATCH

A boat picture on a patch is a fun way to brighten up the back of a child's denim jacket. You can use the same idea to cover a worn area on jeans or dungarees. You'll need a child's garment, a well-washed 6in (15cm) square denim patch, scraps of five mini-print fabrics, plus the sewing and stencilling materials listed on page 48.

Applying the patch

Appliqué and stencil the denim patch, following the instructions on page 49. Embroider the picture in the same way, but use just one strand of cotton (floss) throughout. Then use ecru cotton (floss) to work running stitch all around the design, ⅜in (1cm) in from the edge of the patch. Fuse bonding fabric on to the wrong side of the patch, trim all around it neatly with a pair of sharp scissors, then fuse the patch on to the child's garment. Machine stitch all around with navy thread for extra strength.

BOATING BADGE

This badge uses the small boat motif. Appliqué and embroider it on to a 2¾ x 2in (7 x 5cm) patch. Fuse felt on to the back and stitch around. With Rust cotton (floss), work a straight stitch down each edge; add a brooch pin.

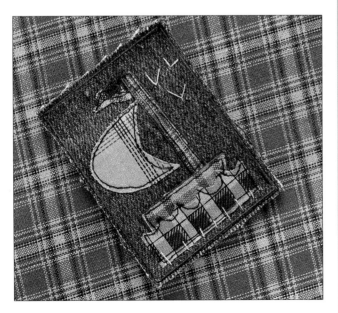

BRIGHT IDEAS

MINI FLOTILLA

A row of the small boats, stencilled in two shades of blue, makes a breezy flotilla sailing across the bottom of a child's T-shirt. Satin stitch the pennants in bright red cotton (floss), and stem stitch pale blue waves below the hulls.

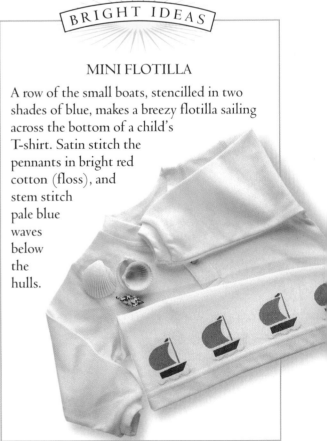

MICE

CHEEKY LITTLE MICE, RUNNING, DIVING INTO
POCKETS AND NIBBLING A LUMP OF CHEESE,
MAKE BRIGHT HIGHLIGHTS ON TOUGH PLAYWEAR
FOR THE VERY YOUNG.

MICE OUTFIT

A cheeky trio of mice stencilled and simply stitched brightens a hat and dungarees set.

Denim dungarees are a fashion favourite for rough-and-tumble children and a sunhat is a summer-time necessity. Here is a cute way to change plain chain-store garments into playtime favourites with playful stencilled mice.

On the dungarees, a cheeky mouse dives into a back pocket to steal a nibble of cheese and, on a front leg, sits eating it. On the hat, a mouse scampers around the band. A little embroidery adds detail to the mice.

Preparing the stencil
You will be using the cutouts shown in colour (below). To make it easier to stencil the running mouse diving into the pocket, cut the stencil to separate the two mice with their ear, nose and eye cutouts. Spray mount the back of the stencil and allow to dry.

Preparing the fabric
Slip the card into the dungarees to prevent paint seepage. Protect the top of the back pocket with a piece of paper folded over the top edge.

PAINT COLOUR GUIDE

For the bodies and tails: add a little Mouse Grey to White to make light mouse grey.

For the eyes and noses: use Mouse Grey straight from the pot.

For the ears: mix White with Bengal Rose to make pale pink.

For the cheese: mix White with a little Fawn to make mid yellow.

STENCILLING THE MICE

1 Position the running mouse cutout with the front feet just inside the back pocket. Mask off to reveal just the body and the tail and stencil with light mouse grey. Allow the paint to dry. ▲

2 Align the nose, eye and inner ear cutouts over the stencilled mouse. Masking off as required, stencil the nose and eye with Mouse Grey, and the inner ear with pale pink paint. ▲

3 Stencil the sitting mouse on the front of the dungarees as in steps **1-2** (left). Remask to reveal the cheese cutout. Align it over the mouse's lower front foot and stencil it with mid yellow. ▲

4 Keeping the hat flat, position the running mouse cutout on the hat band and stencil it as in steps **1-2** (above). When all the paint is dry fix it with a hot iron. ▲

EMBROIDERING

Refer to the stitch details and use single strands of thread throughout. Add outlines to the bodies with stem stitch, then work the tail with slanted satin stitch. Fill the inner ear and cheese with long and short stitch.

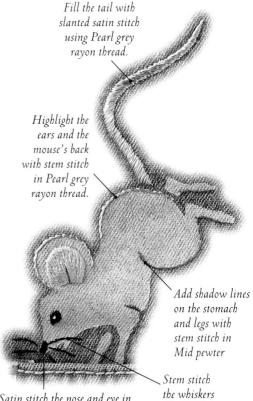

Fill the tail with slanted satin stitch using Pearl grey rayon thread.

Highlight the ears and the mouse's back with stem stitch in Pearl grey rayon thread.

Add shadow lines on the stomach and legs with stem stitch in Mid pewter

Stem stitch the whiskers using Black.

Satin stitch the nose and eye in Black and add a French knot in the centre of the eye using Pearl grey rayon thread.

Fill the inner ear shape with long and short stitch using Pale dusty rose.

Complete the ear with a single straight stitch in Mid pewter.

Work the cheese in long and short stitch using Pale old gold yellow.

MOUSE PATCH

A furry mouse makes a sweet decoration for a baby's plain top. The mouse is stencilled on white cotton fabric, embroidered fully for a realistic furry effect, and stitched in place with decorative running stitches.

YOU WILL NEED

- ❊ A baby's plain white top
- ❊ Stencil and stencil brush
- ❊ White cotton fabric, 8in (20cm) square
- ❊ Stencilling and stitching equipment as listed on page 52
- ❊ DMC stranded cottons/floss and rayon threads as listed in the colour key
- ❊ White sewing thread

COLOUR KEY

COLOURS	SKEINS
Stranded cotton/floss	
■ 310 Black	1
▨ 318 Dark pearl grey	1
▦ 415 Pearl grey	1
▦ 761 Pale dusty rose	1
▦ 3822 Pale old gold yellow	1
Rayon thread	
▦ 30415 Pearl grey	1
▦ 30762 Pale pearl grey	1

Preparing the stencil

You will be using the sitting mouse, alternative tail and the eye, nose, inner ear and cheese cutouts. Before you start, mask off any nearby cutouts. Spray mount the back of the stencil and allow it to dry.

STENCILLING AND STITCHING

1 Centre the sitting mouse on the fabric and mask off the tail. Stencil the mouse, its eye, nose, ear and the cheese as in steps **1-2** and **3** on page 53. Align the alternative tail and stencil it with light mouse grey. When all the paint is dry, fix it with a hot iron. ➤

2 Mount the fabric in the hoop and embroider the mouse, referring to the stitch details (below) for colour placement and stitches. Work with single strands of thread throughout.

3 Trim the patch to 4¼in (11cm) square with the design centred. Press in a ⅜in (1cm) hem all around. Secure in place on the top with running stitches and three strands of Pearl grey.

Satin stitch the outside of the ear in Pearl grey rayon thread. Fill the inner ear with Pale dusty rose and add a straight stitch with Dark pearl grey.

Satin stitch the back ear and leg with Dark pearl grey.

Stem stitch shadow lines on the ear and front leg using Dark pearl grey.

Stitch the whiskers, nose and eye as shown on page 53.

Fill the body with long and short stitch with the stitches running down the length of the body.

Start on the back with Dark pearl grey, blending into Pearl grey and then Pale pearl grey rayon thread on the stomach.

Fill the cheese with long and short stitch using Pale old gold yellow.

For a furry effect, add straight stitches over the cotton using Pearl grey rayon thread.

Work the tail in slanted satin stitch using Pearl grey rayon thread.

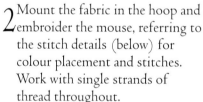

CHILDREN'S SLIPPERS

These colourful felt slippers are cosy and lightweight and very easy to make. The soles are strengthened with insoles cut from sew-in pelmet interfacing, and the sides and back are elasticated to help keep them on lively feet.

Choose a bright colour for the outers and a contrasting colour for the linings. Alternatively, cut the outers and linings from one colour, and embellish the outer pieces with stencilling, embroidery or a jolly felt appliqué design.

The trace-off patterns are on page 80. When making up the slippers, take ¼in (6mm) seam allowances throughout. There is no need to neaten seam allowances because felt does not fray. The finished slippers are continental sizes 22-24.

CUTTING OUT

Trace off the patterns including any dots and marks. For the back upper only: fold the tracing paper, trace the outline with the dotted line on the fold, turn the tracing over and trace the other half.
From the outer felt: cut two back uppers and two front uppers.
From lining felt: cut two front uppers, two back uppers, and four soles.
From pelmet interfacing: cut two insoles. Make a tailor's tack at each dot.

MAKING THE SLIPPERS

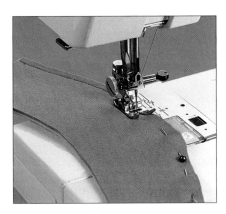

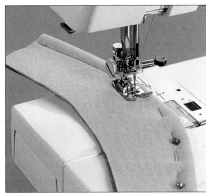

1 Stitch each outer back upper to a lining back upper along the outer curved edges. Snip the curves and turn right side out. Press the seam.

2 Stitch ⅜in (1cm) below the seam to form a channel for the elastic. Tack the raw edges together below the channel.

These pink felt slippers are stitched with lilac thread to highlight the toning lilac linings.

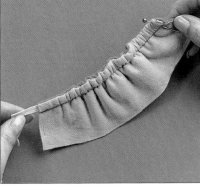

3 Cut two 3½in (8cm) lengths of elastic. Thread the elastic through each channel with the bodkin. Pin then tack the ends in place.

TO41080

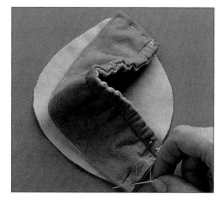 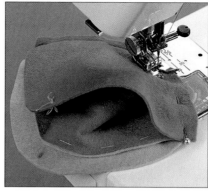 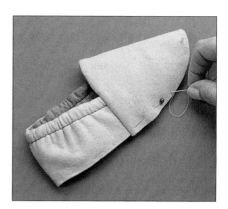

4 With the slipper outers together, pin and tack the short ends of the back uppers to a front upper, matching the lower outer edges.

5 Pin the slipper inner front upper on top, and stitch the layers together along the upper edge, enclosing the back uppers. Snip the curves.

6 Turn right side out and press the seam. Tack the raw edges of the front uppers together.

 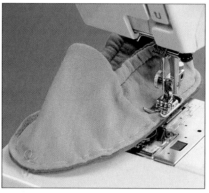 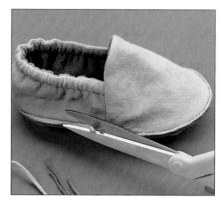

7 Glue the insoles centrally to a pair of soles – flip one sole and insole to make a pair. Apply the glue evenly and sparingly so it does not seep through the felt. Leave to dry. Pin then tack the remaining sole on top.

8 Pin and tack the uppers to the sole, matching the front dots and the side dots to the seams. Stitch in place.

9 Trim the seam allowance ⅛in (3mm) from the seam.

HANDY HINTS

NON-SLIP SLIPPERS
If you have slippery floors, you can make the slipper soles more slip-resistant by adding a layer of a non-slip material such as suede. Simply cut two soles from the material and tack them over the felt soles in step **7** (above).

Two complementary colours work well for these slippers.

FLAP PURSE

This cleverly designed purse is extremely versatile. You can make it any size you like – just adapt the specifications given in the caption below.

The purse is fully lined and the seams are machine stitched. The lining is cut in two pieces – when you join them, leave a gap in the seam to turn the bag through. You can secure the flap with a popper, as shown overleaf, or, alternatively, use a decorative closure, such as a frog fastener, as shown left, or a button and loop.

For the best results, choose closely woven fabrics for the main piece and the lining. Cottons and linens are easy to work with; silk and satin are more difficult to handle but give a luxurious feel.

If you want to embroider or appliqué your purse, embellish the main fabric before assembling the pieces. For a quilted bag, cut the lining to size after quilting the main piece, as quilting can 'shrink' fabric.

To make a purse with a straight edge, simply miss out step **1** (below). Follow the remaining steps, working with a rectangular-shaped main fabric and larger lining piece.

Decide on the finished width (**A**), height (**B**) and depth of the flap (**C**) for your purse. **From your main fabric:** cut a piece **A** plus 1¼in (3cm) by twice **B** plus **C** plus 1¼in (3cm). **From lining fabric:** cut one piece **A** plus 1¼in (3cm) by **B** plus 1¼in (3cm). Then cut a second larger piece **A** plus 1¼in (3cm) by **B** plus **C** plus 1¼in (3cm).

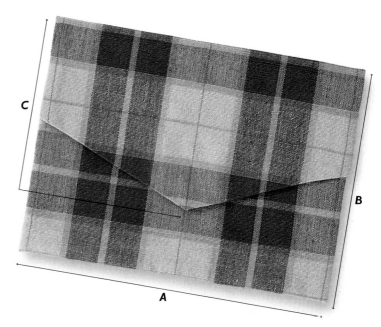

SHAPING THE FABRIC PIECES

1 For a pointed flap, fold the main fabric piece in half lengthwise. Decide how deep to make the point, and mark this measurement on the long raw edge. Draw a line from the mark to the top of the fold. Cut along the line through both layers. Repeat with the larger lining piece.

2 Trim off ³⁄₁₆in (2mm) all round both the lining pieces. This ensures that the lining will sit comfortably inside the bag without wrinkling.

ASSEMBLING THE FLAP PURSE

1 Stitch the lining pieces right sides together along the bottom edge. Take a ⅝in (1.5cm) seam and leave a 4in (10cm) gap in the centre. Press the seam open.

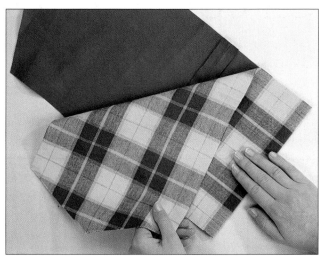

2 Stitch the lining and main fabric right sides together along the short straight edge, taking a ⅝in (1.5cm) seam. Trim the seam, then turn it over and press to form an edge.

3 Fold up the front edge, right sides together, to the depth **B**, so the lining seam with the gap is at the base. Bring the lining from the back, enclosing the folded front edge, so right side lining lies against right side main fabric. Pin to hold.

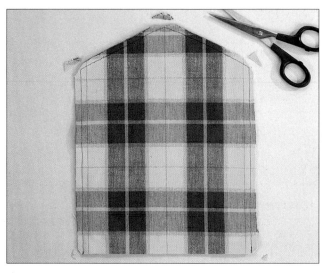

4 Stitch through all the layers along the sides and round the pointed top, taking a ⅝in (1.5cm) seam. Trim the seams and corners. Then turn the purse out through the gap in the lining seam.

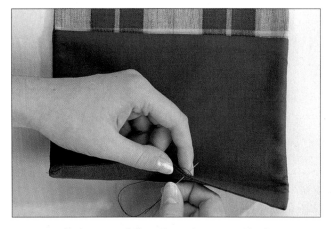

5 Press the bag carefully. Close the gap in the lining with slipstitches. Use a matching thread and fasten off the ends securely.

6 Turn the bag right side out and press. Use chalk to mark the positions of the two halves of the popper on the front and the inside of the flap. Stitch the popper in place.

CIRCULAR-BASED BAGS

Circular-based drawstring bags have lots of storage potential. Small ones are handy for toiletries and hosiery, while larger duffle bags are ideal for sportswear and beach gear.

This bag measures 10in (25cm) tall. To make a pattern for a different sized bag, draw a circle with a diameter the desired width of your bag. Measure the circumference with a fabric tape measure. Draw a rectangle the length of the circumference by the desired height of the bag. Add ⅝in (1.5cm) seam allowances all around.

Use closely woven fabrics for the main bag and the lining, matching sewing thread, cord, pins, tacking thread and paper.

MAKING A SMALL BAG

1 Use a compass to draw a 7½in (19cm) diameter circle on paper, cut it out and draw around it on to the fabric. Mark a 21¼ x 11in (54 x 28cm) rectangle on the fabric for the side piece. Cut out both pieces.

2 Fold the fabric rectangle in half widthwise, right sides together, and pin the short side edges. Stitch, leaving a ⅝in (1.5cm) gap for the casing, ¾in (2cm) from the top edge. Press the seam allowances open.

3 With the right sides together, pin and tack the base to the lower edge of the bag. Stitch, then remove the tacking. Clip the curves with sharp scissors.

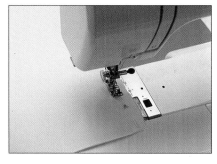

4 Make a second bag in the lining fabric, following steps 1-3, omitting the gap in the casing and leaving a 5in (12.5cm) gap in centre of seam to turn through when bag is assembled. Turn lining the right way out.

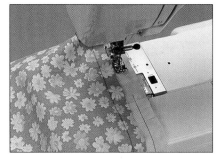

5 Slip the lining into the bag, so that the right sides are together. Pin then stitch the upper edges. Turn the bag right side out through the opening. Slipstitch the opening closed and press the upper edge.

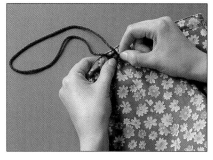

6 For the casing, stitch close to the upper edge and then ¾in (2cm) below. Cut a 44in (110cm) length of cord and use a safety pin to thread it through the casing. Knot the ends together and hide the knot in casing.

MACHINE APPLIQUE

Machine stitched appliqué is strong and durable, so it's ideal for embellishing items that get a lot of wear and tear and require frequent laundering. The most popular technique is bonded machine appliqué, shown below. With this method you fuse the appliqué motifs to the background material with a bonding fabric, such as Bondaweb (WonderUnder). This keeps the motifs securely in place while they are stitched, so there's no need to use pins. The motifs are stitched with a close zigzag stitch, also known as satin stitch.

The bonding fabric makes it easy to achieve smooth and professional results. It prevents the motifs from fraying, so there is no need to turn under the edges. It also stiffens the motifs slightly, making them easier to cut out and stitch. It is sold in packets in fabric and craft shops and department stores.

Stitch the motifs with either matching or contrasting thread, depending on whether you want a sophisticated or bold finish. You can use ordinary sewing thread or, for a more decorative look, machine embroidery thread. Use your normal sewing machine foot, or try an appliqué foot. These are made of clear plastic so it's easy to see the stitching.

Bondaweb (WonderUnder)

Machine embroidery threads

Cutout motifs

Sewing threads

Appliqué foot

PREPARING MOTIFS

1 Select the motif you want to use and cut it out roughly. Leave a margin of about 2in (5cm) around the outside of the motif.

2 Cut a piece of Bondaweb (WonderUnder) slightly smaller than the cutout motif. Place it rough side down on the wrong side of the motif. Press with a medium hot, dry iron to fuse the materials together. Use a pressing motion rather than sliding the iron.

3 With the right side of the fabric uppermost, cut out the motif accurately, using small, sharp scissors.

SEWING BOX

CUTTING OUT

To save time when you're cutting out several motifs from the same piece of fabric, iron a sheet of Bondaweb (WonderUnder) on to the back of the fabric before cutting out the motifs. Then cut roughly round each motif and trim the outlines accurately with small sharp scissors, as shown in steps **2-3** above.

STITCH LIBRARY

THIS CHAPTER CONTAINS ALL THE STITCHES USED IN THE PROJECTS, GROUPED TOGETHER FOR EASE OF REFERENCE.

SATIN STITCH

Starting and finishing off satin stitch

When you have finished satin stitching a motif, always secure the thread ends and trim them off before working the next motif. Don't trail the thread across the back of the work to start another motif – it may show through as a shadow on your finished work, especially on lightweight or pale fabric.

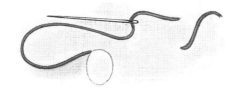

1 A little way from your starting point, push the needle through to the back of the fabric, leaving a 3in (7.5cm) tail of thread on the right side. Bring the needle out to the front again at your starting point on the edge of the motif.

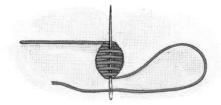

2 When you have filled in the motif, take the thread through to the back. Weave it into the back of your stitching, and trim it off close to the surface. Then pull the first thread end to the wrong side, weave it in and trim it off in the same way.

Filling a rounded shape with basic satin stitch

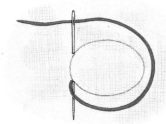

1 Bring the needle out at the front of the fabric at the edge of the shape. Insert the needle at the opposite edge, and bring it out again next to where you started.

2 Pull the thread through gently, so that it runs straight between the marked lines without wavering; it should lie smoothly against the surface of the fabric, without puckering it.

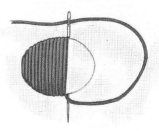

3 Repeat steps **1-2**, keeping the stitches parallel and close together so that they lie neatly and evenly on the surface of the fabric.

Working a basic satin stitch line

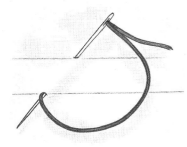

1 Bring the needle out at the front of the fabric at the lower marked line. Take the thread upwards and insert the needle on the top row, at a 45° angle to the marked line; bring it out again next to where you started.

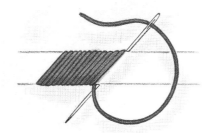

2 Work parallel, closely spaced stitches along the row, keeping them at exactly the same angle and placing the needle precisely on the marked lines to create even edges.

Loose stitches
Loose, untidy satin stitches are created when working the stitch over an area which is too large. For the best results, each stitch should be no more than ⅜-½in (10-12mm) long. For large areas use encroaching satin stitch, worked in manageable rows.

STRAIGHT STITCH

Securing your starting thread

Finishing off

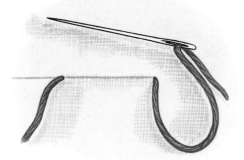

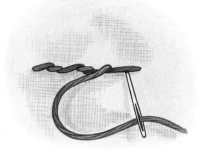

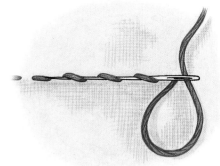

1 Push the needle to the back of the fabric, a little way from your starting point. Leave a short tail of thread at the front. Bring the needle to the front at your starting point.

2 As you work along the line, stitch over the thread at the back to secure it. Then pull the loose thread end through to the back and snip it off close to the surface.

To secure the thread end when you have finished, push the needle to the back of the fabric. Weave the thread into the back of several stitches and trim it off close to the surface.

Working basic straight stitch

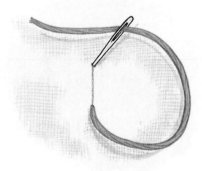

To work an individual straight stitch, bring the needle out to the front. Push it through to the wrong side to make a single stitch of the required length.

To work a cluster of straight stitches, work individual straight stitches of varying lengths and in different directions according to the design.

To create a simple straight stitch flower, make as many straight stitches as desired, working outwards from a central circle or oval.

Working running stitch

Working backstitch

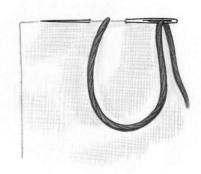

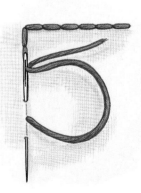

Working from right to left, bring the needle out to the front at your starting point. Pass the needle in and out of the fabric along the stitching line. Work several stitches at a time, keeping the length and tension even.

1 Working from right to left, bring the needle out to the front one stitch length from your starting point. Insert the needle at your starting point and bring it out again, two stitch lengths away.

2 Pull the thread through to leave a single stitch at the front. Then repeat step 1, inserting the needle in the hole at the end of the previous stitch. Continue in this way, keeping all the stitches the same length.

Working stem stitch

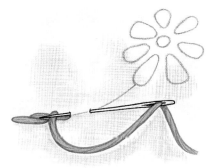

1 Work upwards, keeping the working thread to the right. Bring the needle out to the front and insert it a little way from your starting point. Bring it out again, half a stitch length back.

2 Insert the needle half a stitch length from the end of the previous stitch. Bring it out at the end of the previous stitch, through the same hole in the fabric. Continue in this way.

For a heavy stem stitch line, angle the needle slightly as you insert it, and work smaller stitches.

FRENCH KNOT

Starting and finishing knotted stitches

When you are working individual knots or widely spaced knots, fasten off the thread after each knot. When working groups of closely spaced knots, you can carry the thread across the back of the fabric between knots, instead of fastening it off after every stitch.

To start, work two or three tiny stitches at the back of the fabric, positioning them where they will be covered by the embroidery stitch. To finish, fasten off the thread in the same way, directly beneath the knot. Trim the thread close to the fabric.

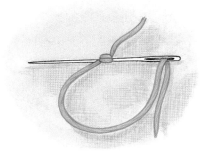

Working a French knot

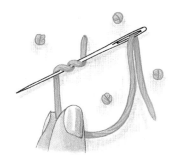
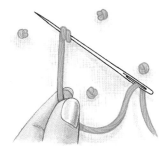
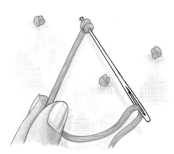

1 Bring the thread through to the front of the fabric. Holding the thread taut with your left hand, wrap it twice round the needle.

2 Pull the thread gently to tighten the twists round the needle. Don't overtighten the twists, or you will find it difficult to slide the needle through in the next step.

3 Keeping the thread taut, insert the needle into the fabric close to the point where it originally emerged. Pull the needle and thread through to the back, to leave a loose knot at the front.

FLY STITCH
Working fly stitch

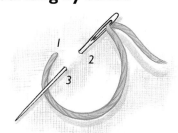
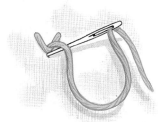
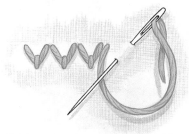

1 Bring the needle to the front at 1. Insert it to the right at 2. Angle the needle and bring it out over the working thread at 3.

2 Pull the needle through and make a vertical stitch over the loop to anchor it to the fabric.

3 To make a horizontal row of fly stitches, bring the needle to the front at the top right of the first stitch and repeat steps **1-2** along the row.

BLANKET STITCH

Securing the thread

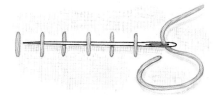 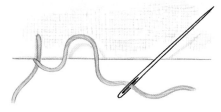 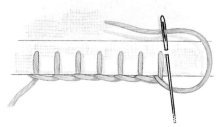

Method A Push the needle through to the front at your starting point, leaving a short tail of thread at the back. Work a few stitches, then turn the fabric over and weave the loose thread into the back of the stitches. To finish, fasten off the thread in the same way.

1 Method B Use this method for edging appliqué and fabric edges. To start, insert the needle at the top edge of the stitching line, leaving a tail of thread at the front. Take the working thread over the loose thread, ready to work the next stitch.

2 Work the row of stitches, then take the thread to the back. Make two or three tiny stitches on top of each other, next to the last upright and taking the needle through the background fabric only. Finish off the thread at the start in the same way.

Working blanket stitch for surface embroidery

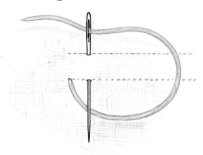 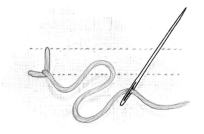 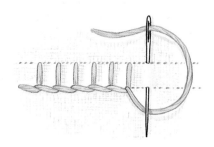

1 Bring the needle to the front on the lower line and insert it at the top, a little way to the right. Bring it out directly below, keeping the thread under the tip of the needle .

2 Pull the thread through the fabric, over the top of the working thread. Gently pull the thread to form a firm loop at the lower line.

3 Continue working in this way, spacing the upright stitches evenly and making them all the same height.

Working blanket stitch as an edge for appliqué

Tack or fuse the fabric shape in position. Blanket stitch round the edge keeping the stitches you are working towards you. Work the top of the uprights through both fabrics and bring the needle out to the front just outside the edge of the shape, through the background fabric only.

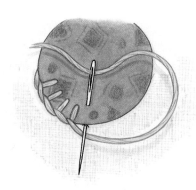

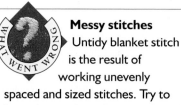 **Messy stitches** Untidy blanket stitch is the result of working unevenly spaced and sized stitches. Try to keep the stitches of an even length and space them out at equal intervals along the row.

Finishing a fabric edge

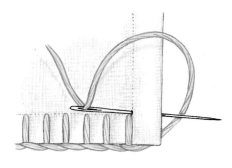

Work blanket stitch along the fabric edge, positioning the loops on the edge of the fabric. To turn a corner, stitch up to the corner, then insert the needle at the same point as the last upright. Bring it out at the perpendicular edge, carrying the thread under the fabric.

LONG AND SHORT STITCH

Working long and short stitch

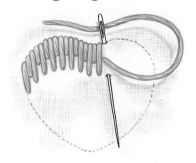 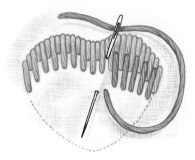

1 Work the foundation row in alternate long and short stitches, working from left to right and following the outline of the shape to be filled. Work the stitches close together.

2 Work the second row from right to left, filling in the spaces left by the first row and keeping the stitches all the same length.

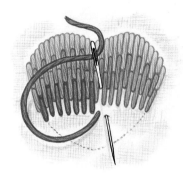

3 Work subsequent rows alternately from left to right and right to left, keeping all the stitches the same length, as in step **2**. Change thread colour as you work for a subtle blended effect and work stitches closely so no background fabric shows.

TURKEY STITCH

Working Turkey stitch

1 Take the needle to the back at the bottom left of the shape at 1 and bring it out to the left at 2, leaving a 2cm (¾in) tail of thread at the front. With the working thread above the needle, make a horizontal stitch to the right at 3. Bring the needle to the front again at 1 and pull the thread through.

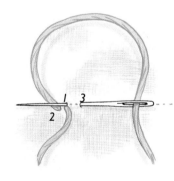

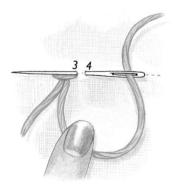 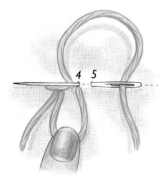 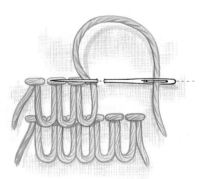

2 With the working thread below the needle, make a short horizontal stitch from 4 to 3. Pull the needle through gently, holding down the working thread so that it forms a small loop below the line of stitching.

3 With the working thread above the needle, make another short stitch from 5 to 4. Pull the needle through to complete the stitch.

4 Repeat steps **2** and **3**. At the end of the row, take the thread to the back and fasten it off. Work the next row above the first row, following steps **1-3**. When the shape is filled, use a small pair of scissors to cut the loops, if required.

COUCHING

Starting off couching

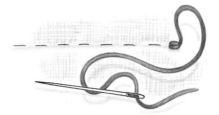

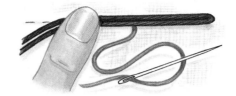

1 Start at the right hand end of the couching line. Secure the couching thread first with a few backstitches. Place them where they will be covered by the laid thread. Leave a 2in (5cm) tail of thread at the back of the fabric.

2 Place the laid thread on the fabric, leaving an extra 2in (5cm) at the start of the couching line. Hold the laid thread in place with your left thumb.

Finishing off couching

To finish off the couching thread, take it to the back of the fabric. Secure it with a few stitches beneath the laid thread. Leave a 2in (5cm) tail of couching thread. Then cut off the laid thread, leaving a 2in (5cm) tail.

To secure a fine or mediumweight laid thread, thread the end on to a large-eyed needle and gently take it through to the back of the fabric. At the back, fold the end over the row of stitching. Then secure it with a few stitches, using the couching thread.

To secure a thick laid thread, make a small hole in the fabric with a large needle or the point of a stiletto. Wrap sticky tape round the end of the laid thread and poke it carefully through the hole and pull it to the back. Secure as for a fine or mediumweight thread.

Working basic couching

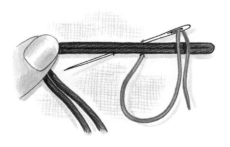

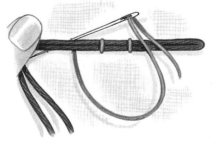

1 If you are using two strands of laid thread, fold a single length in half and position it on the fabric with the strands side by side. Bring the couching thread to the front, just below the laid thread. Make a tiny vertical stitch over the laid thread. Bring the needle to the front again a short distance to the left.

2 Continue making vertical stitches over the laid thread until it is anchored to the fabric along its length. Space the stitches evenly.

CROSS STITCH

Working individual counted cross stitch

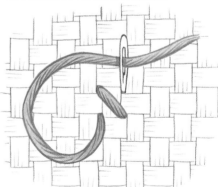

Bring the needle out at the front of the fabric and insert it one hole down and one hole to the right. Pull the thread through. Bring the needle out one hole to the left and insert it one hole up and one to the right.

STENCIL LIBRARY

All the materials you need to make the stencils are available from art and craft stores. It's best to use acetate because it lasts longer, you can see through it and it is easy to clean. Either trace the patterns, which are given actual size, directly from the book on to the acetate using a pencil, or use a photocopy. Tape the paper pattern (if applicable) and acetate on to a cutting mat to prevent it sliding around, and start cutting out the stencil, following the lines. Use a small to medium craft knife or a scalpel with a new blade. Take extra care when cutting around corners and when cutting out the more intricate parts of the design. Remove all the cuttings and you are ready to get stencilling. You can enlarge or reduce a design on a photocopying machine. When using your stencil, there is no right or wrong side. Some designs call for an image to be reversed – to do this, simply flip your stencil, having first made sure it is clean and dry.

If you're using the stencil motif as an embroidery outline, use a very sharp, hard pencil which will leave a fine line on the fabric, or an air-soluble pen, or a thin permanent marker. Water-based fabric paints are ideal for painting through the stencil. Some darken slightly as they dry.

Use stencil brushes to apply the paints. These have stiff, blunt-cut bristles and come in different sizes – the smaller the cutout, the smaller the brush should be.

The best fabrics for stencilling are smoothly woven, natural fabrics. It is best to wash the fabric first to test for shrinkage and colourfastness, and to remove the finish on the fabric. Suitable fabrics include cotton, cotton mixes and linen.

YOU WILL NEED

* Acetate, cutting mat, craft knife or scalpel
* Fabric, washed and ironed
* Fabric paints, including white
* Stencil brushes
* Sharp, hard (H) pencil
* Masking tape
* Lining paper
* Spatula for mixing paints (optional)
* Old white saucer
* Paper towels

Outlining a stencil design

Lay the fabric out on a flat surface and secure it with strips of masking tape. Position the stencil and hold it firmly in place with masking tape. Using a sharp H pencil, draw round the inner edges of the cutout area, keeping the line as light and fine as possible. Alternatively, use an air-soluble pen – the marks will disappear in a few days.

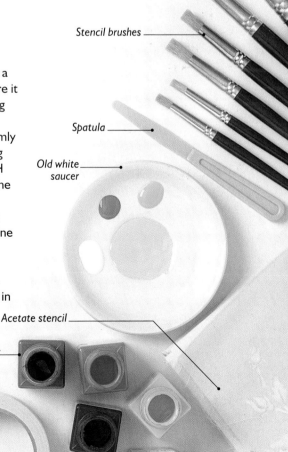

Stencil brushes
Spatula
Old white saucer
Acetate stencil
Fabric paints
Masking tape

Using the Stencils

Before you start, wash the fabric to remove any manufacturer's finishes. Cover the work surface with scrap paper or lining paper to prevent the paint staining it, then stretch the fabric taut before starting to stencil it.

Using the stencil

Stencil all the cutouts in the first colour before applying the second colour. Clean and dry the stencil and brush before applying each new colour. To avoid smudging the paint, lift the stencil off the fabric rather than sliding it off.

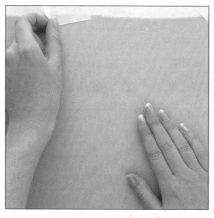

1 Cover the work surface with lining paper. Lay the fabric over the paper and smooth it out. Hold the fabric taut with strips of masking tape.

2 Use masking tape to cover all the cutout areas on the stencil you don't need for the first colour. Tape the stencil firmly in place.

3 Dip your brush in the paint and work it on the saucer until it is quite dry – avoid loading too much paint on the brush.

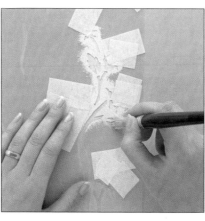

4 Using a firm up and down movement, dab the first colour through the cutout, starting at the outer edges and working inwards.

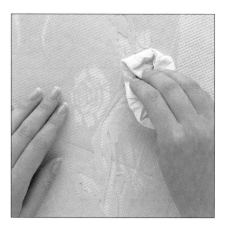

5 Remove the stencil and take off the masking tape. Clean and dry the stencil with water and a paper towel. If the paint is difficult to remove, scrub it gently with an old toothbrush.

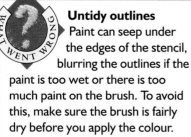

Untidy outlines
Paint can seep under the edges of the stencil, blurring the outlines if the paint is too wet or there is too much paint on the brush. To avoid this, make sure the brush is fairly dry before you apply the colour.

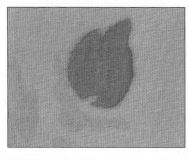

6 If any cutouts you *don't* need for the second colour butt up close to the second colour cutouts, mask them out. Leave a few areas unmasked to help you reposition the stencil, then apply the second colour as before.

7 Allow the paint to dry thoroughly. To set the colour, place a piece of kitchen paper on the paint and press it with a hot iron, according to the instructions provided by the fabric paint manufacturer.

Using Fabric Paints

Depending on how you apply the paint through the stencil – dry-brushing, stippling or sponging – you can create three completely different finishes to suit a range of embroidery stitches.

Dry brushing For a light, streaky finish which adds texture to areas which will remain unstitched, apply the paint with dry brushing.

Stippling For a background of solid colour, suitable for filling stitches such as satin stitch, use a brush to stipple on the paint.

Sponging For a speckled finish, suitable for a wide variety of stitches, apply paint with a sponge.

Materials

Brushes and sponges For dry brush and stippling, use a good quality stencil brush. For sponging, natural sponges are best. They are expensive, but you will only need a small one.

Paint palettes Art and craft shops sell ceramic and plastic palettes for mixing the paints on. Some old white saucers or small bowls cost less and will do the job just as well. Using an old brush, a flexible plastic palette knife, or a small wooden stick to mix the paints, will help avoid damaging your stencil brush, or clogging it with paint. Old teaspoons are useful for dishing out the paints from the jars.

Testing the colour
Getting the colour of the paint right is very important. The steps on page 70 explain how to do simple colour mixing, and how different fabric colours affect the paint colour. You should always test your colours and practise your techniques before starting to stencil. Use a piece of the same fabric for testing the paint colours.

Stippling the paint gives even coverage.

Dry brushing gives a lighter effect.

Sponging the paint gives a speckled finish.

Applying paint through a stencil

Stippling Use a stencil brush to apply the paint with a firm up and down movement. The paint should sink into the fabric, rather than simply coating the surface.

Dry brushing Dip the tip of the stencil brush into the paint, and dab off the excess on kitchen paper until the brush is nearly dry. Stroke it across the cutout to create a light film of colour.

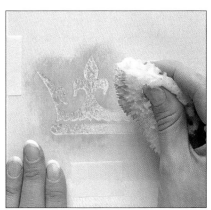

Sponging Dip the sponge in the paint and squeeze it almost dry. Dab off any excess paint on a scrap of paper, then dab the paint lightly through the stencil cutout.

Making a pastel colour

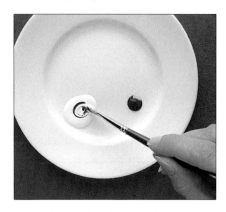

1 Put about 1 tbsp (15ml) of white paint on the saucer. Swirl in a tiny dab of the main colour.

2 Mix the colours with a small brush or a flexible palette knife, then test the colour on a spare piece of fabric.

3 Dry the paint with a hairdryer before checking the colour – the paint darkens as it dries. Add more white or coloured paint, as necessary.

Making a dark colour lighter

1 Put about 1 tbsp (15ml) of the main colour on the saucer, and add in a tiny dab of white paint.

2 Mix the paint, then test the colour on a spare piece of fabric. Dry the paint as shown above.

Fabric paint colours can look very different depending on the amount of white you mix in. The fabric strips below show four different colours, each mixed with progressively larger amounts of white.

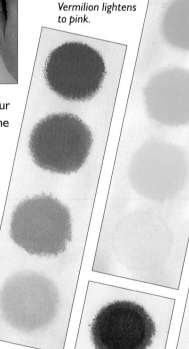

Vermilion lightens to pink.

Gold yellow rich creamy undertones

Deep brown mixed with white becom lilac.

Turquoise blue loses its strong green tones, reducing to a delicate shade of aqua.

Choosing the right colour

Always test the paint colour on your fabric before starting to stencil, as the fabric colour can alter the paint colour. Colours are truest on white (above right). On mauve, for example (below right), the same colours look drab. For clearer paint colours on coloured fabrics, add a little white to the paint.

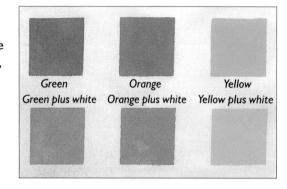

Green
Green plus white

Orange
Orange plus white

Yellow
Yellow plus white

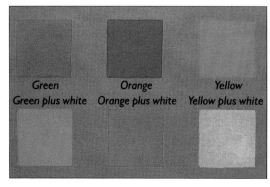

Green
Green plus white

Orange
Orange plus white

Yellow
Yellow plus white

TEMPLATES

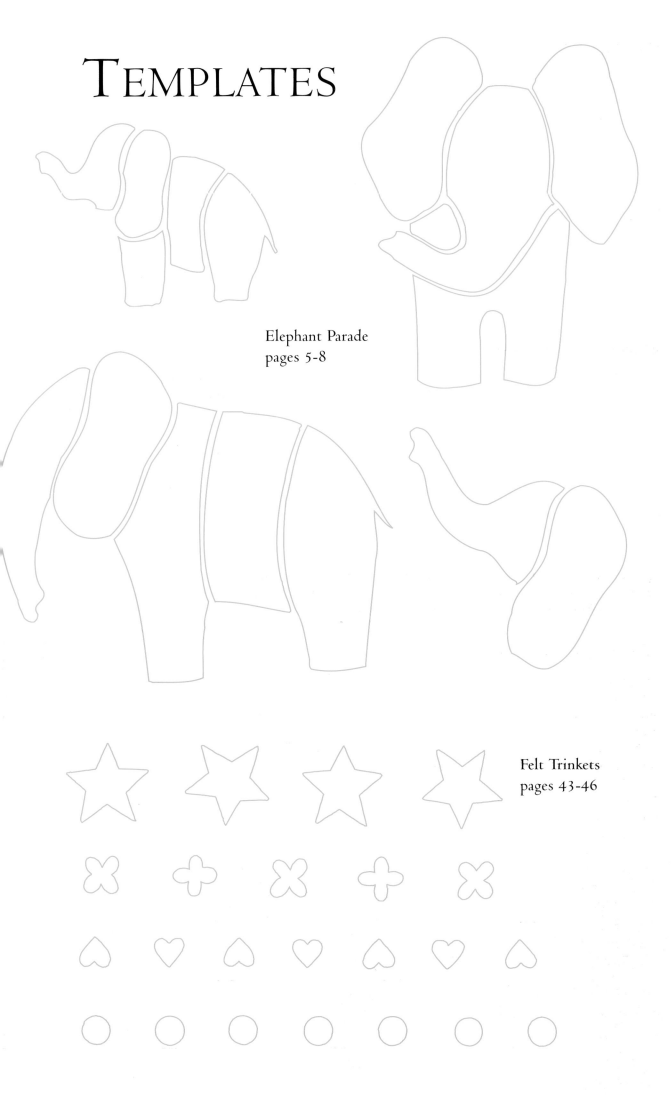

Elephant Parade
pages 5-8

Felt Trinkets
pages 43-46

72

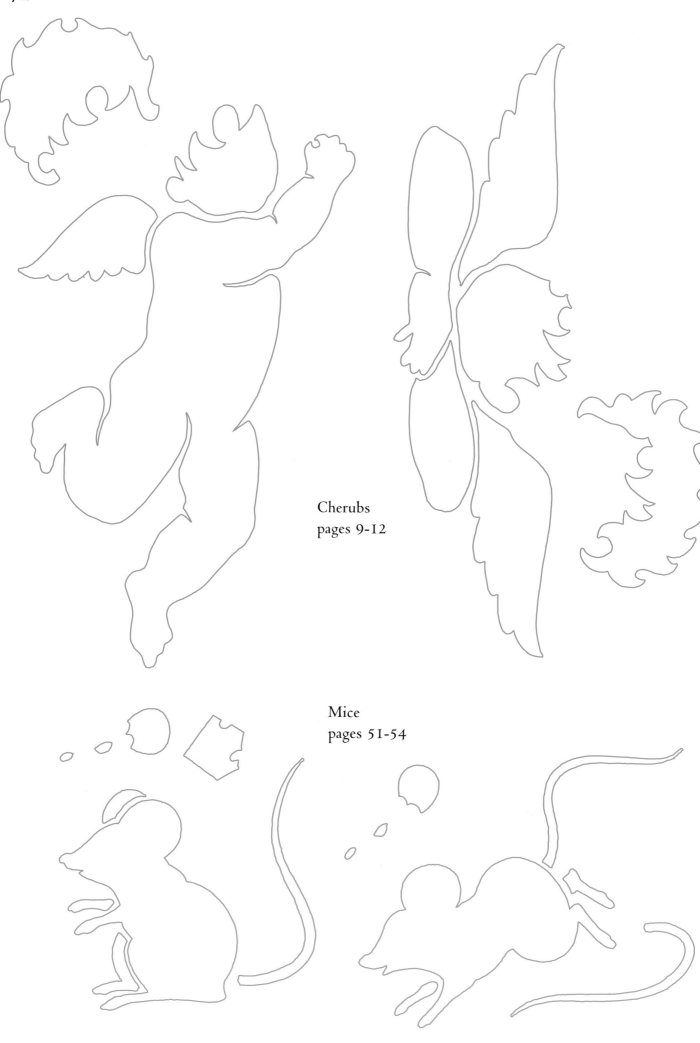

Cherubs
pages 9-12

Mice
pages 51-54

Macdonald's Farm
pages 13-16

Sail Away
pages 47-50

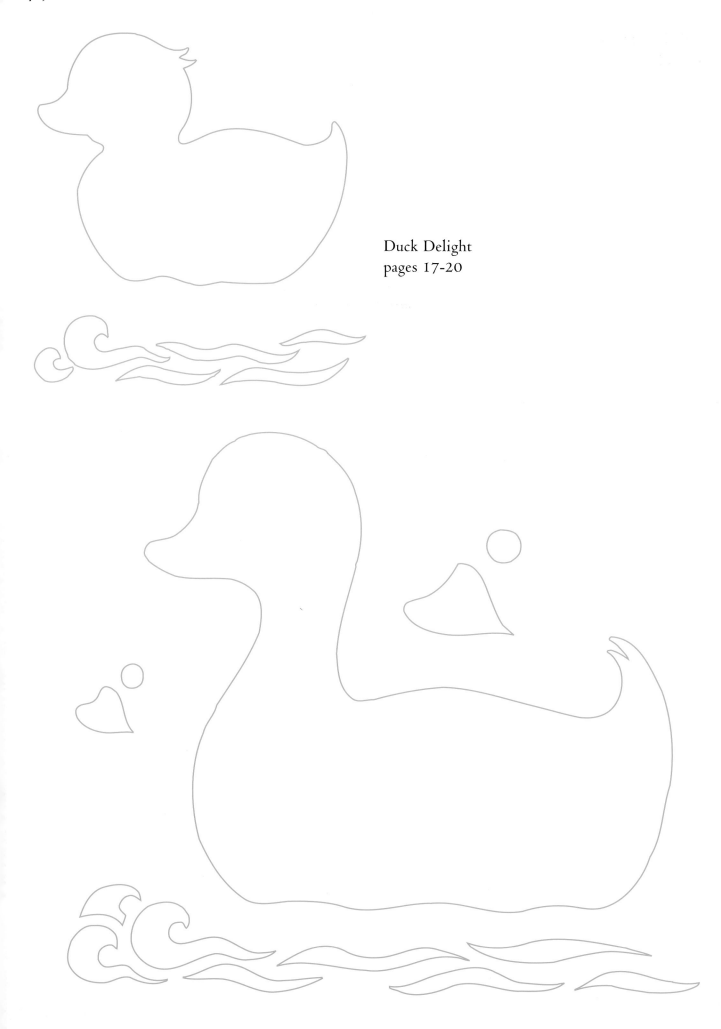

Duck Delight
pages 17-20

Rabbit Slippers
pages 39-42

Teddy Bears
pages 21-24

Big Cats
pages 25-30

Cuddly Sheep
pages 35-38

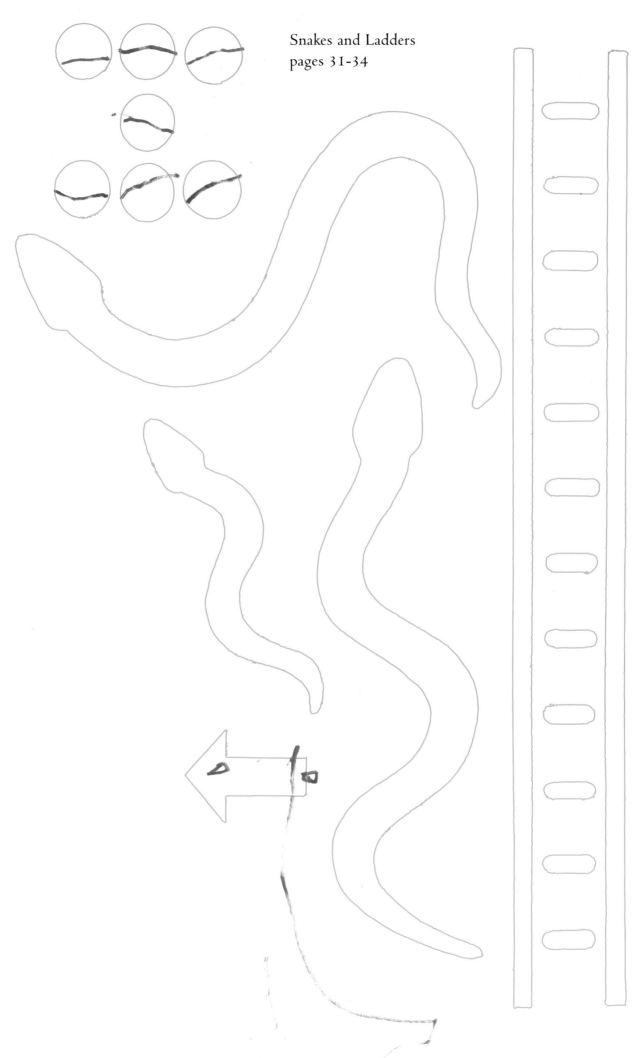

Snakes and Ladders
pages 31-34

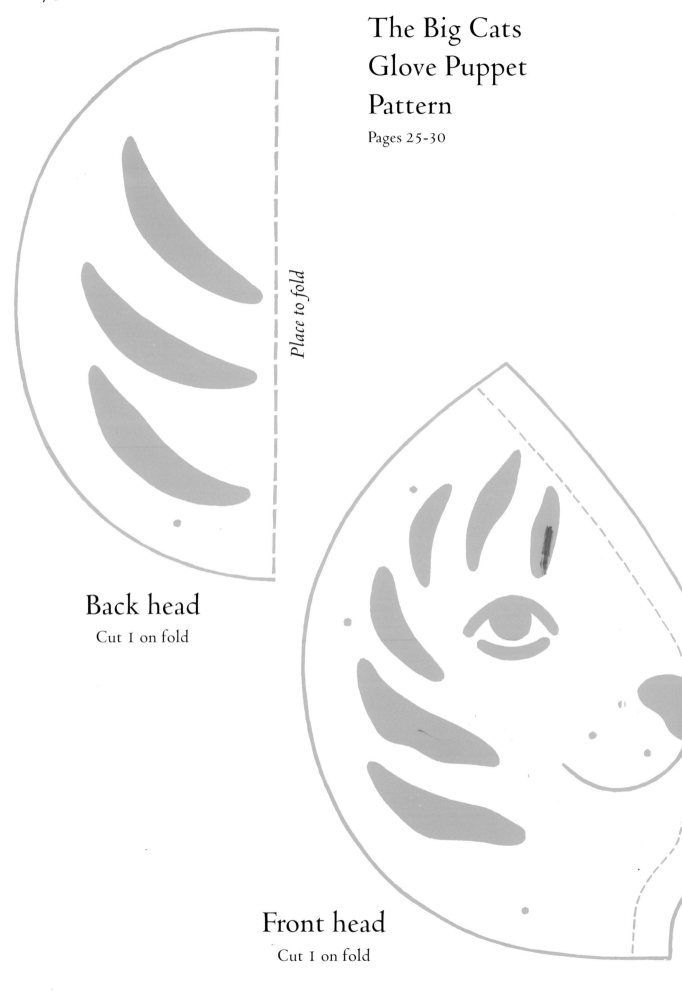

The Big Cats Glove Puppet Pattern

Pages 25-30

Place to fold

Back head

Cut 1 on fold

Front head

Cut 1 on fold

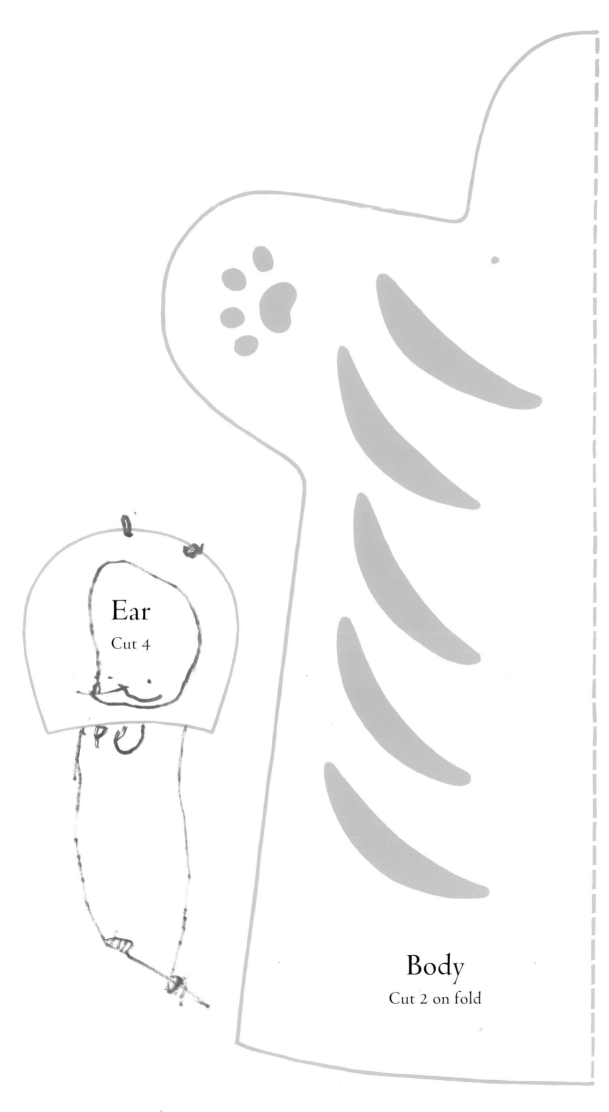

Place to fold

Ear

Cut 4

Body

Cut 2 on fold

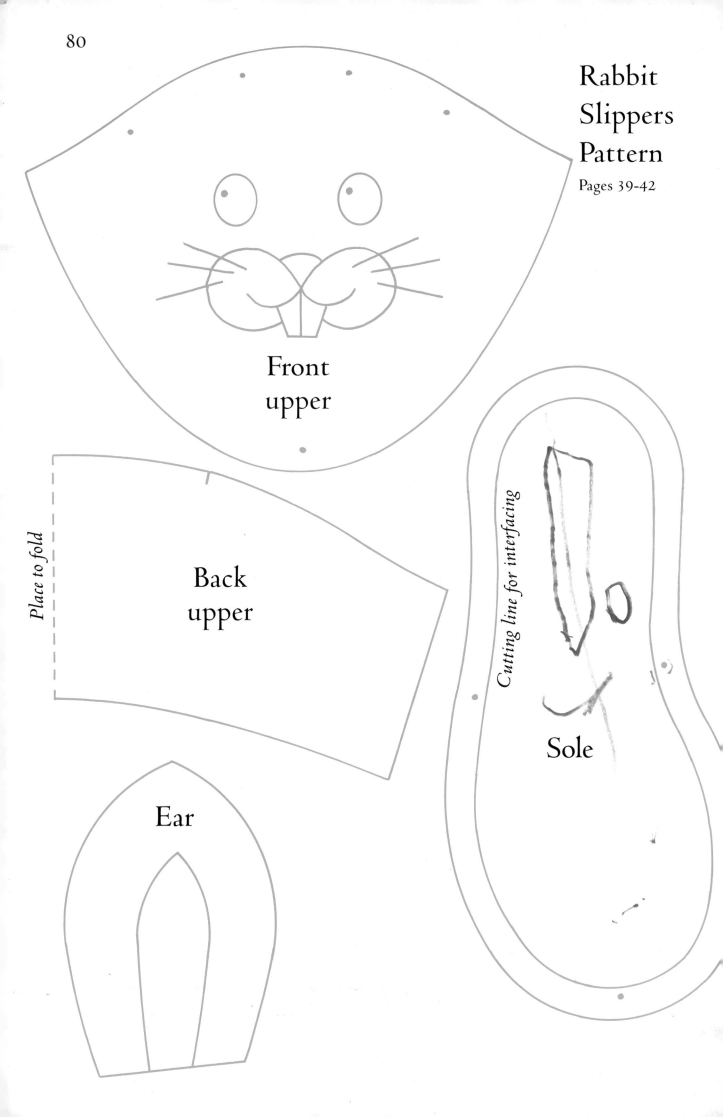

Rabbit
Slippers
Pattern
Pages 39-42

Front
upper

Place to fold

Back
upper

Cutting line for interfacing

Sole

Ear